Searching Soul for Truth & Light

Marva Samuels

Searching Soul for Truth and Light
Copyright © 2008 by Marva Samuels

All rights reserved. No portion of this book may be reproduced in any form or by any electronic or mechanical means; photocopy, recording, and scanning or other, such as or including information storage and retrieval systems without permission of author. The only exception by a reviewer who may quote excerpts in a review.

Cover design and book design by Barron Steward

Photography Credits
pages #: 3-6-11-16-17-21-31-92-110-112-115; Personal photos of my family and friends on events and vacations
pages #: 121-127-136-139-141-144-145; Two African Maasai Tribes' photos featured with permission of both Maasai Chiefs while on vacation in Tanzania, Africa 2006
page #: 20-154; My granddaughter beside an angel and a stained-glass feature of "God is Love" with permission of owner of the Biblical Gardens, Grass Valley CA
pages #: 119-147; Myself with African masked-man dancing; myself with African drummer drumming; and myself, Christina, and African Maasai warrior at craft store with permission of all persons while on vacation in Tanzania, Africa 2006

Printed in the United States of America
First Printing
ISBN – 13: 978-0-9892594-0-8

ACKNOWLEDGEMENTS

I give thanks to GOD foremost; my angels, spiritual teachers, guides, totems, and ancestors that have contributed to this book and to making it a reality. God, your unconditional love allowed me to penetrate my heart and soul to seek the authentic self and release my baggage of shattered emotions.

To understand my sensitivities I experienced Native American Spirituality. Here with the help of my instructors, Elaine and Robin, I experienced my creative writing talents. Their encouragement led me to explore counseling for my anger, pain and trust issues. Thank you for your time, support, and love at that seasoned time.

Lou thanks for yours praise of my work and accepting it for editing at such a stressful time for me. You lifted my spirits and brought me joy. Barron, thank you to the best creative artist and graphic designer ever.

To Lasonja, thanks for my first edit, JoAnne thanks for helping with my flash drive and my computer, Judy L. thanks for you for helping me create my book photos album, Karin thanks for final edit, Angela thanks for fine-tuning and aligning my graphic design, and special thanks to Phillis for book consultation.

Special thanks to my family especially, my deceased mother, my deceased maternal grandmother, my son, Jesus, and my brothers Clinton, Clifford (aka Joe), Milton, and Mark for their love and support. I also thank my daughter-in-law, Nina, for her time with photos. I thank my grandchildren Jahron, Jaimoni and Jailah for just being you. I love you.

Now, let the journey begin.

I dedicate this book to my grandmother, Gladys Thorne, and my mother, Bernice Samuels.

FOREWORD

It has taken me many years, since 1977, to actually publish my journey of penetrating my soul. This book was written from divine spiritual healing. Sometimes, just a word, other times a phrase, or a sentence was whispered in the silence. Repetition would continue until I stopped what I was doing and used my creative feminine energy to write.

I first started writing poetry in 1977, voicing my opinion of the injustice of racism, destruction of Mother Earth, pollution of Father Sky, disparity of social, political, and religious differences. My story was rage and my warrior was in full-military attire against the issues of white and black and rich and poor. In the stillness and silence I released my feelings of fear, pain, anger, sadness, love, joy, peace, and happiness. This catharsis touched my soul. My inner being lit up!

The inner flame grew and glowed radiantly as my authentic self blossomed with self-love with Great Spirit at my side. As we talked and talked, my soul connected to Great Spirit. Slowly, in 1998 I softened along my journey and began the awakening and discovery of self-empowerment and transformation.

As I awakened, I discovered a deeper strength and power, full of love, kindness, forgiveness, and compassion, which surprised me with a new breath of life and a new beginning.

A transformation, my soul connected to God. Here, I present my soul at its best, with God at my side; I give to you all the love I have as I share my soul for truth and light.

Table of Contents

Book Cover Photo
Copyright
Acknowledgements
Dedications
Foreword

Family	2
My Grandmother's photo	3
Nanny, My Love	4
Mom, My Special Person	5
My Mom's photo	6
Joy and Happiness	8
My Son's and Mom's photo	9
Goodbye, featured by my son	10
Author and Mom's photo	11
The Final Goodbye	12
Daddy I Love You	13
Waterfalls (my tears)	14
From A Boy, To A Man, featured by my son	15
My Son's and Grandson 's photo	16
Author's and Son 's photo	17
Jesus My Love	18
Innocence	19
Granddaughter 's photo at Biblical Gardens	20
Grandson's photo playing in park	21
Let's Have Fun	22
Gift or Burden	23
No More, No More	24
A Mislead Soul	25
Thanksgiving	26
Christmas Time	27
Burney Falls photo	29
Spiritual	30
Author's photo	31
Egotism	32
Money	33
Anger Can Change	34
Why Do I Struggle	35
Love	36
Loving Thoughts	37
Woman	38

Womanhood	39
United	40
Stone Wheel	41
Racism	42
Cleansing	43
After The Storm, Rainbow photo	44
What Is Change?	45
Creative Mind	46
Mt. Shasta photo	47
Serenity	48
My Special Journey	49
A Gift Of Love	50
Burney Falls photo	51
Anchor	52
My Home	53
Walking In Balance and Harmony	54
God Above All	55
Mt. Shasta photo	56
In The Silence	57
African Tree, Tanzania photo	59
Truth	60
Redwood Trees photo	61
Above And Beyond	62
Mt Shasta photo	63
Sacred Mountain	64
Elk in Redwoods photo	65
Nature's Beauty	66
Earth Healing	66
Summer Day	68
Redwood Tree (brotherhood) photo	69
The Redwood Trees	70
Medicine Man	71
Mother Earth	72
Dear Heart photo	74
Long Dance	75
Purification	76
Apophylite	77
The Light	78
The Sun	79
Full Moon	80
I Weep	81
Haiti	83

Journey	86
The Beginning	87
Scenic picture	88
Awakening	89
Calling	90
American River, Auburn, CA photo	91
Decisions	92
Spirits Come Alive, photo Cayman Islands	93
Burden Lifted	94
To My Truth	95
1998	97
January 1999	98
Death Arrow 1999	99
Beyond The Shadows	100
Releasing The Chains	101
Geyser, Napa CA photo	102
Evolution Day	103
Sexual Abuse	104
My Precious Baby	105
What Time Is It?	106
LOVE IS ALL I NEED	107
Soul Within	108
Loving Self	109
Author, rally in San Francisco photo	110
Do It Now	111`
Author, Oahu, Hawaii photo	112
Soul Retrieval	113
Soul-Love	114
Author at home photo	115
The Glow	116
Known Encounters	117
Friendship	118
Author dancing at craft store, Arusha, photo Tanzania vacation 2006	119
African Hotel photo while vacationing in Tanzania, Africa 2006	120
African Maasai Sisters photo, vacationing in Tanzania Africa 2006	121
Sisterhood	122
Lion Pride photo while vacationing in Tanzania Africa 2006	123
Rites of Passage	124
Wildebeest photo while vacationing Serengeti, Tanzania 2006	125
Freedom	126
Author dancing with Maasai women photo Tanzania Africa 2006	127
Is It Really Me?	128
I Am	129

I Am Whole	130
Back Together	130
Agreements	132
Letting Go	133
Open To Receive	134
Balance And Harmony	135
African lion photo while on vacation in Tanzania, Africa 2006	136
A New Breath Of Life	137
The Dove	138
African Child photo vacationing Tanzania, Africa 2006	139
When I Was A Child	140
Maasai Couple photo, vacationing Tanzania, Africa 2006	141
Africa	142
Sisters Of The Dance	143
Dancing with Maasai Sisters photo vacationing Tanzania Africa 2006	144
Maasai children photo vacationing Tanzania Africa 2006	145
Joy And Radiance	146
Author, Christina, Maasai Warrior photo vacationing, Tanzania, Africa 2006	147
Tolerance	148
Author/African school children photo vacationing Tanzania Africa 2006	149
We Are One	150
Peace At Last	151
God is Love photo Biblical Gardens, Grass Valley CA	153
The Key Of Life	154
Scenic photo	155
In God We Trust	156

Vocabulary words
Author's Note
Author's Bio

FAMILY

Next to God, family is the most important thing to me. Here in the family chapter of the book, "Searching Soul for Truth and Light", I have written four personal poems related to my grandmother, mother, father and son. Other poems relate to individual problems and issues, plus family time.

Hopefully, you can feel the love of family no matter what the issue. We all know that family can take one on a roller-coaster ride of emotions of loving, liking and hating. All of these emotional changes bring us closer together. It is this family bond of love that creates value and family blessing.

Many blessings to you and your family and may God Bless You.

NANNY, MY LOVE

Nanny, I miss and love you so much.
I remember the times of our special moments,
while I rode your stationary bike
and you rested on your bed;
We shared our deepest feelings of self and family.
Those discussions bonded our hearts and souls
in a love bundle of peace, joy, and happiness.
Other times, we bonded in silence
as you sat in your living room chair
and I sat at your feet with my head in your lap
hugging your legs, while you tenderly caressed my hair.
These were our special moments of loving, caring, and sharing together.
It's difficult to release you to Great Spirit.
I miss and love you so much.
But my spiritual growth says
it's time to release you in the physical plane
and receive you in the Great Mystery
and let my magic flourish and my creative energies flow.
As I rise to my fullest potential
I ask you to be my spirit guide in The Void
for the love, security, and protection we shared.
For the everlasting bond of love.
So I reach out to you and let you know
I have released you to Great Spirit
with all my love
From the depths of my heart and soul,
I LOVE YOU NANNY.

HO

MOM, MY SPECIAL PERSON

Mom, you are such a special person to me.
You have been there through ups and downs,
joys and woes,
But you have never changed.
That nurturing spirit that caresses my being,
your smile of joy and assurance,
the inner turmoil of letting go
always with the hope everything will be all right,
brings love and joy to my heart and soul.
Your prayers to Great Spirit
to watch over me
guide me,
protect me,
surround me,
with the pure, white light.
Have given me faith and trust in Great Spirit.
I have learned well
through your example and good intentions and I
thank you
and I love you
From the depths of my heart and soul.

HO

Searching Soul For Truth and Light

JOY AND HAPPINESS

It was all arranged.
A surprise of a lifetime,
Mom's surprise birthday party.
At age 72,
winning the lotto one week ago
brought joy and happiness.
But nothing compared to that precious night of November 26, 2000.
The quiet dinner arranged with one of her sons.
But behind her back
a family birthday bash was planned.
Arrangements were made for the sons, grandchildren, and great-grandchildren to come together in celebration.
Celebration of the matriarch of a family
Honor, respect, and gratitude flowing
conference call arranged with the brother and sister out of town.
The moment planned to perfection.
Mommy was surprised.
But the joke was on all of us.
We were all surprised.
Because there he stood,
Bold, Black, and Brave,
her favorite child,
her baby,
who flew over 3,000 miles
for that special precious moment in time,
Tears flowed.
The room glowed radiantly with the white light.
A family coming together
for the moment of an Elder's recognition
for a job well done
Celebrated on this Evolution Day.
Love flowed freely and abundantly.
A precious moment of joy and happiness
Joy and Happiness!
Joy and Happiness!
The cup runneth over, love flowed.
Joy and Happiness!

HO

Marva Samuels

GOODBYE

Its seems like yesterday you were here
visiting your grandson and great-grandchildren.
Some days I think I see you sitting in my chair
smiling big
as you see me playing with the children;
I'm loving every minute of it.
But as the thought of you goes
I smile now,
because the memories of you are sweet, cheerful, and peaceful.
Even though you passed 11-08-05,
It seems like yesterday;
Even though I did not get to say goodbye the way I wanted to.
I missed being at your funeral due to unavoidable circumstances.
So I'll say now,
Goodbye Grandma,
I love you and miss you always.
To show my love was deep
I tattooed your portrait on my arm,
so that I would be blessed with your presence always and forever.
As the days grow easier
and my will stronger in my day-to-day tasks
let me say from my family and me,
Thank you for the memories.
And that I love and miss you.
Grandma, Goodbye with love
and when my day comes,
may you open the gates with my mother,
So that I can say *hello and I love you*.

You're loving Grandson
JESUS RENE SAMUELS

Marva Samuels

THE FINAL GOODBYE

As I walked
I felt numb.
Knowing death was final
the anticipation of facing Mom
in the final stage
Was heart-breaking.
Lifeless she lay.
But she expressed peace and serenity
joy at last
for a soul
Returning home
Mom always expressed
God is the answer.
Now, God was the answer
as He claimed His child
and brought her home.
Sitting on the prayer steps facing Mom
I expressed my love for her and what her love meant to me:
unconditional love, respect and honor, wisdom, stability
dependability, always being there, teaching me, setting the example,
unity of family, loving God, and all other things.
There is nothing like a Mom
Once lost,
The hole in your heart is deep.
But remember the life,
memories of old.
Love is deep
family of the utmost
faith and belief in God
For the final goodbye
That last kiss
That last touch
As I cried,
releasing my sorrow
I bent down
and kissed and hugged my Mom
for the last time.
Feeling and touching her hair,
the only life left in her,
I said,
my final goodbye,
I love you Mom.

HO, YOUR LOVING DAUGHTER MARVA

DADDY I STILL LOVE YOU

At the time it was hard to believe those things were happening to me.
Molestation and physical abuse by my dad.
It always happened when my brothers, you, and I were playing,
wrestling on the floor, laughing together.
Times of fun, joy, and confusion.
How could you do those things to your favorite child?
The statement "You're not a good Dad." would always be cried out.
My confusion and disgust would only bring a smile to your face
and laughter from your voice.
On one of your drunken nights you almost did the unthinkable.
But God was on my side.
Standing in my room one night your stares woke me up.
The look on your face made me get up and run swiftly to my mom.
Mom woke immediately to my cries, "Daddy! Daddy! Daddy!"
She comforted me. She arose and found you.
Suddenly reality hit and your drunk was over.
Mom took me back to my room and comforted me 'till I fell asleep. Whatever
happened or whatever was said between you and Mom was never
mentioned. But I do know you never touched me again.
There seemed to be shame and sadness in your eyes.
I understand the burden of abuse with your dad,
Never a kind word,
Always cruelty,
The constant physical and emotional abuse,
Your dad demonstrated to your mom over and over again,
left you in a state of confusion.
No excuses. You were responsible for your actions.
It almost cost you the love of your wife and daughter.
It left me with a complete lack of trust in men.
But I understand your burdens are not my burdens
and I must lift those burdens to Great Spirit
for the Oneness and Godliness of Self.
My heart is opened to receive that special person now,
while my soul is full of forgiveness and love.
So Dad, rest in peace.
Because I forgive you and love you from the depths of my heart and soul.

HO

FROM A BOY, TO A MAN

Mother's Day: a day to remember,
A day to look back and say
Whoa!
What a wonderful Mom I have.
The woman who took on any challenge
and the biggest challenge of all
raising a boy into a man.
What a job you did instilling in me
Such cherished values that I live by today
Such as:
standing tall
believing in what I say
and standing by my word
helping a boy turn into a man.
I know it was difficult.
Especially, with a knuckle head like me
but you have succeeded
by ensuring that I set goals, for myself to reach
so when reaching the goals we could be proud together
To sit and bask in the accomplishment.
To honor you in one day is unheard of
But this day is to cherish and appreciate what you've done for me
Turning a boy into a man
and giving me the only gift I need from you
My life, December 25, 1976.
Marvelous Marva Ann Samuels
You are loved, cherished, and put on a pedestal
Not just for Mother's Day, but for every day of the year
because it didn't take one day
To Turn A Boy Into A Man.

      Love Always, Your Son
      JESUS RENE SAMUELS

Searching Soul For Truth and Light

Marva Samuels

JESUS MY LOVE

My son,
I am so proud of you
You are my special person.
My heart skips beats sometimes
and at others times it beats too fast.
My love for you is full of joy;
you excite my inner energies
and bring in the love of a dove.
Let go of your old ways of the past
And go forth to the new creative energies you have
within. Don't block your energy
let your positive energy flow.
And lift your burdens to Great Spirit
lightening your load;
and give thanks
for your lessons and blessings;
and know that your dreams are a reality
of burden or freedom.
The choice is yours.
The world is what you create.
All things are possible.
The journey is without limits.

        MOM,
          MARVA SAMUELS

INNOCENCE

Innocence is a pure virtue.
Like the lamb of God
Without blame, guilt, or corruption.
It's as precious as a newborn baby,
with the aura of a saint.
This state is a child's sanctuary.
A place of impeccable behavior, trust, safety, and love.
Guardianship and protection are of the utmost.
Children look to parents to protect them from harm
because they are unable to comprehend the meaning of right and wrong.
As life progresses and one matures,
innocence depicts a virgin, naiveté, and simpleness.
Innocence means a clear conscience void of negativity, violation, and profanity.
Innocence means seeking your inner spiritual being
for purity of heart and soul
and deliverance from burdens and victimization.
To become a female of strength, courage, and power
with the innocence of a child
and the flavor of trust, purity, honesty, and respect
For harmony, balance, peace, joy, and happiness.

Searching Soul For Truth and Light

LET ME HAVE FUN

Let me have fun
Let me enjoy the beauty
of the open fields, plains, meadows, and valleys
With the vibrant green grass and many different-colored flowers.
As I take a deep breathe and smell the scents of nature,
I feel the caress of the gentle winds on my face
And the solid foundation of the earth beneath my feet.
The strength and power of Father Sky
The loving nurturing nature of Mother Earth
Touch my heart as I hear the many sounds of the birds and animals.
Be still and listen.
Inner Self is calling.
Peace, joy, and serenity calm me
helping me remember myself as a child
riding the bike,
jumping rope,
running in the wind,
feeling the warmth of the sun on my body and face
playing with my brothers and friends
enjoying the moment
No thoughts or senses of tomorrow.
So Great Spirit, as I walk my path
I ask that you guide and protect me
so my inner children feel the joy and freedom of playing again.
For peace, joy, love, and happiness
and foremost for my healing and wholeness again,
Let's play and have fun!

HO

GIFT OR BURDEN

Is it a gift or burden?
Whatever it is I'm scared.
Take it away!
Take it away!
I fear it.
My life is consumed
with the images of people I know.
Take it away!
I don't care.
Listen, be calm for a minute
and let me explain.
You have a gift.
It's not a gift.
It's a burden.
However, you see it,
It carries responsibilities of helping others.
Don't let your fear block your blessings.
Face your fears through meditation.
Ask Great Spirit
for assistance in controlling your intuitive psychic energy,
So, you are in charge of turning it on or off.
Don't block your blessings.
Help me!
Help me!
Seek God in counsel during meditation and prayer,
and ask for what you need.
Drum, rattle, and play the piano
Flow with the energy of your music.
Feel the beat of your heart in unison with the beat of the drum and rattle.
Flow together in rhythm.
Catch you breath and breathe.
Ask for prayer and deliverance
Manifest your fear into the power of your soul within.
Let your soul seek the truth of your visions.
Understand that God is using you as his servant.
Are you strong enough to serve?
Go within your heart and soul and find the answers;
there are no surprises.
You know the answers.
Accept your blessings.
And flow with the energy of Great Spirit
as he unfolds special messages to you.
These messages are meant to be passed on.
You are God's special messenger.
Is it a gift or a burden?
Neither, it is a responsibility.

NO MORE NO MORE

No more
No more
Alcohol a disease
Destroying the physical and psychological.
Ruining the mind and body
shattering my soul.
For years I walked in the fog
not being responsible or accountable for my actions.
Painlessly I strolled.
While my loved ones cried
Stop!
Pain and anger not heard
Feelings were held in the void.
My low self-esteem
let me fear the mirror
No more
No more
Self-awakening and self-discovery
helped me seek help.
Now, with
Nineteen years sobriety,
My celebration.
I'm fearless
Self-empowered
Self-transformed
Full of love, compassion, and forgiveness
lets me feel joy, peace, and happiness
I'm fearless!

A MISLEAD SOUL

A family united for death toll
I wept.
The victim; a cousin, a young soul
An accident
Deliberate
Suspicion no doubt.
I wept,
A family united for a surprise encounter
An aunt once loved and cherished
now, a misled soul.
Recognition; a question, until names
exchanged. Many hugs and kisses
For a love once cherished
My heart pitter-patter,
Jumping for joy
For a love once cherished
Love cut abruptly, for a lie once told
I wept.
A family reunion with a misled soul.
Now,
Face-to-face
With a lie told,
Immediately,
erased the anger and mistrust.
For love conquers all
I wept.
I hugged and kissed
and whispered, *I love you*
to the misled soul
My embrace was accepted
because love conquers all
I wept.
For a misled soul
In my heart and soul
I knew this was the last
The last encounter of love,
with the misled soul I wept.
Tears of sadness
knowing and understanding
this was the last encounter
with a misled soul
I wept. I wept. I wept.
For my love of a misled soul.

THANKSGIVING

We're not going to pass the plate.
We're not going to have Church.
But we *are* going to have Sunday Dinner
On Thanksgiving Day,
A Day of Prayer and Thanksgiving,
a time for caring and sharing,
a family day of love and nutrition,
and a day of giving thanks to Great Spirit
For all our lessons, blessings, and abundance,
A day of riches in love, relationships, experiences, creative ideas, health, and spirituality,
Great Spirit let us give thanks for our unlimited abundance;
For our faith is strong.
And our love everlasting.

HO

CHRISTMAS-TIME

Christmas-time,
a time of thanksgiving
thanking Great Spirit for all of our lessons and blessings.
A time of reflection,
letting go of old negative habits for a lighter, brighter you
a time of empowering self with strength, wisdom, love, and happiness,
a higher energy level of loving self and others
For the highest good of mankind.
A time of giving,
especially to the young, elderly, and those less fortunate than ourselves
a time of good cheer with love, peace, joy, and harmony
this feeling is not just for one day, December 25,
But a feeling for everyday
giving prayer and thanking God for all of our riches and abundance with
the understanding that giving is not only for one,
but for all mankind
Christmas is a time for all
to feel the beauty of the Rainbow Tribe.
This experience is not meant for one day but always.
Christmastime, is our connection to the Oneness and Godliness of Self
and Rainbow Tribe Vision.
Lift up your arms in prayer
and feel God penetrate your soul.
Release your spirit of giving, loving, and sharing with other.
Because Christmastime is every day.

HO

SPIRITUAL

In understanding spirituality, Christianity did not meet all my needs regarding vision and premonitions. These visions and premonitions assisted me in discerning my right path to God Above All.

Native American spirituality is a prerequisite to the heart and soul for some, and a journey to understanding self and accepting God as your Savior.

Nature can be a Church for some, guiding one to the silence, stillness, and serenity of God's Word.

Marva Samuels

EGOTISM

Self is a complex person with many pieces left unknown.
To some, *Self* is well known, well expressed, and well understood.
Nothing can be told or said that isn't known already.
Before a thought can be completed
the individual is saying, very annoyed and with impatience,
I know.
Ego and conceit breed selfishness.
Where every person, place, and object is secondary
to the number one, *Self*
If any person, place, or object is placed first
it is done for an ulterior motive.
Well, if I act this way
or let things be like this
I'll get *this*,
Just what I want.
Hypocrisy and phoniness thrive comfortably in the ego.
Ego never does wrong
or makes a mistake;
It's just unheard of.
Me? Make a mistake!
Oh no!
I think you misunderstood me.
Giving is done always with the definite thought of receiving in return;
when nothing material is returned,
Self is upset and angry,
thinking how selfish the other individual is.
Only *Self* knows what is perfect.
And only *Self* can accomplish exactly what is to be done.
No other individual can show, tell, or suggest another way or idea;
That's simply not heard of.
Questions are never asked.
Everything is understood.
And if anything goes wrong
I know,
It wasn't me.

HO

MONEY

A source of abundance to the right
it is the root of all evil.
Money means wealth.
For a few, money means power to rule and conquer others.
Money is control
For a few
The mind set is:
    I rule the world
    I set the standards
    Which are not meant for me
    They are for others to abide by
    I reign with wealth, power, and control.
Where is the love?
Love, Who needs love?
Money, a source of abundance to the right.
It is a spiritual gift,
a time of caring and sharing
charity of the utmost.
Money is a gift from Great Spirit.
A giveaway that creates lessons, blessings, and abundance.
Money is a Spiritual gift
to assist the poor, crippled, handicapped, and downhearted
to create Spiritual awakening, discovery, restoration, empowerment, and transformation
Money is:
    A lesson of love and charity
    A blessing of give away
    Abundance in the Life forces
    Love, joy, peace, and happiness
Money to the left or to the right
Neither,
I walk in balance and harmony connected to Great Spirit
at the root, core, heart, and soul.
So, in my world,
I have manifested with intention of the highest good:
    Balance and harmony,
    Love and charity
    Wealth and power
With Divine Guidance,
Money is provided in a Spiritual way
as a Spiritual gift.
Abundance
of love and charity.

HO

ANGER CAN CHANGE

Anger is the color red.
Anger is explosive.
Anger is abusive.
Anger is painful
Anger is hurtful.
Anger is negative.
Why do we hurt each other?
Blame, resentment, hate are burdens carried with low self-esteem,
Causing sadness with feelings of depression, hopelessness, and indifference
Things do not have to stay the same.
The world is what we create.
Ask Great Spirit for a white light of protection.
Seek counsel with your totems and each direction
For a change in energy, direction, and creative spirit;
Remember,
Attention goes where energy flows.
There are no limits all things are possible.
Ask with intention.
And what is known to you,
Will be given to you by Great Spirit.
Have faith and pray.
Give honor and gratitude to Great Spirit, Mother Earth, Father Sky,
Four Winds and Four Directions, and Ancestors.
Ask Great Spirit for Peace and Deliverance.
Use your heart chakras and reach your soul.
Seek love, strength, balance, harmony, peace, and joy.
Remember:
Depression will change to happiness,
War will change to peace,
Anger will change to love,
Safe journey.

WHY DO I STRUGGLE

Why do I struggle?
I'm so tired.
I can't take it anymore.
My head is pounding;
frustration and anger are at its highest peak.
Why do I do this to myself?
Constantly screaming and making a tantrum when I'm stressed.
The pressure is in my chest.
When will it stop?
Child, it starts and stops with you.
Your struggles, challenges, and blockages
are your weakness and your strength.
The choice is yours.
Positive action versus negative action,
ego clashing with your heart and soul
Why won't I listen?
Maybe it is time to cry so healing can begin.
Ask for prayer and deliverance;
Great Spirit will never fail you.
Release your fixed ways and chronic complaints.
Open up your heart and soul to receive.
Stop fighting.
Take a deep breath of life and begin in a new way.
Kindness and compassion,
Love and forgiveness,
Peace and joy.
Not everyone will walk your path
and it is these people
who will create a burden that will need to be released.
Cut the cord,
sever the relationship,
walk your walk,
talk your talk,
and speak your truth.
Surround your spirit with those of similarity and feel yourself expand
and grow. Never forget those you leave behind;
the struggle or success is yours.
The world is what you create.
All things are possible.
The possibilities unlimited.
Seek your heart and soul.
Ask Great Spirit for answers
then the struggles will be lifted
and the success will be yours.

LOVE

Love is purity.
Love is rich.
Love is emotion.
Love is joy.
Love is everlasting.
Love is a feeling of enrichment.
Loving one's self brings peace, joy, and happiness.
Balance and harmony of male and female energies,
Coming together of Mother Earth and Father Sky
Reaching for that eternal feeling in the pure white light
Lifted burdens to lightness and buoyancy
Bringing one closer to everlasting love
Feeling that Oneness with Great Spirit.
Loving within and without.
I strive to cross the bridge, Great Spirit.
Love, peace, joy, and happiness are yours.
Wherever you are,
The world is what you create.

LOVING THOUGHTS

Missing you more than words can say.
My authentic self,
My soul, vividly creates a picture in my mind
making me remember the long, harmonious walks I used to take.
Slowly I strolled along the earthly path,
with the ancient trees arranged in their pattern of growth.
Calmly, the beautiful, bright green leaves swayed on their
branches flowing with the wind,
as the sun brightly shone
giving light and life.
In the distance,
the tranquility of the river is seen,
with only the movement
of the tiny flowing ripples.
I select a bench
I sit.
Here I meditate and envision a reflection of me,
trying to ease or erase the headache I've created.
I lovingly stroke my face and massage my temples tenderly.
Inwardly, to myself,
I pray to Great Spirit to help me shed my outer shell
so I can become the woman I AM.
Within and without
hurt and pain were the cause of my stubbornness
as well as my insecurities and uncertainties
in not knowing what the outcome would be.
Scared me to death,
but now is the moment of my power.
I understand,
Power comes from within.
The world is what you create.
There are no limits all things are possible.
Attention goes where energy flows.
Effectiveness is the measurement of truth.
And love is to be happy with one.
These principles
assisted my healing, transformation, and empowerment
So now
acceptance is as is.
Non-judgmental attitude,
and detachment of the utmost,
always has me remembering to send
Loving thoughts.

WOMAN

Woman;
A creation of God
a nurturing, loving, and caring person
always following her heart.
Her emotions and intuition are heartfelt
with intention for the highest good of mankind
Seeds are planted.
Fruit is manifested.
A world is created.
A world of spiritual love,
spiritual awakening, discovery, restoration, empowerment, and transformation
Woman;
A Spiritual Warrior
bears children
That she nurtures and loves for a lifetime.
She sets the tone for generations to come,
making a strong foundation
with unconditional love, guidance, and protection.
Woman;
Sets the tone
Sets the pace
So awake, my sweet beauty
It is now time to advance and go forth
There is much work to be done.
Now is your moment of power.
All things are possible
so create your world
with Great Spirit at your side
A world of:
        Love and Joy
        Peace and Happiness
        Balance and Harmony
        Equality and Unity
        Life and Wisdom
Woman:
A Spiritual Warrior
A loving and nurturing soul
A beautiful sweet creation of God
Sets the tone
Sets the pace
For the world that she creates.

HO

WOMANHOOD

I am woman
God's love
A reality
Giving breath of life to new beginning
A gift of life
A gift of love
      A Journey;
Along a Sacred Path
A time of love, joy, and peace
A time of play, fun, and laughter
      A Journey;
Of sadness
With loss of innocence, trust, and safety
A sense of lost security
Walking on shaky ground
Feeling the sadness, turmoil, and uncertainties
      A Journey;
Searching to be whole again
A time of silence, stillness, and strength
A self-awakening
A self-discovery
Going within to the flicker of the lit flame
A time to face my fears,
To walk in balance and harmony
A time of respect, trust, truth, and honesty
A time to connect with soul
For the Oneness and Stillness of Great Spirit
A time to be in the present
      A Journey;
Now,
feeling my empowerment and transformation
Created my strength and power
As I walk
As I AM
For the woman I was
For the woman I AM
For the woman I am to be
I thank Great Spirit
For all my lessons, blessings, and abundance
For my soul connection to the God Head
I glow radiantly
Into my womanhood
because
I AM.

UNITED

I stand tall
my feet firmly grounded with Mother Earth.
I feel the warmth and love
as she caresses and nurtures me
She sets the tone
so,
I flow
with the rhythm and beat of her energy.
Together
United
As One,
We flow and glow
Radiantly.
I give thanks and praise to Father Sky
as I connect to Great Spirit.
What time is it?
Time to unite
Soul and Self,
a Spiritual Union.
What do I need?
Trust, truth, respect, and honesty;
Faith in Great Spirit;
Self-awakening, self-discovery, self-empowerment, self-transformation Soul-Love
So
Let your authentic self

    Shine!

    Shine!

    Shine!

STONE WHEEL

Stone Wheel,
slowly turning 'round and 'round
never missing a beat
making a solid foundation
of strength and power
creating a new world.
Transformation,
channeling of new ideas
will be rooted
and bring fruit.
A time of joy
with abundance of love, peace, and happiness.
Respect and gratitude
will ignite the flame within
so my soul will glow
in the authentic light
feeling the warmth and love of Great Spirit.
My soul unites with the Goddess Head.
My chakras in balance
I glow brightly
all colors
coming from all directions.
Life-forces alive and well,
fill my secret garden
with many flowers
different colors
different sizes
different shapes
a place of serene divinity.
Stone Wheel,
turning 'round and 'round
A solid foundation.

HO

RACISM

Years of oppression, for people of color, Third World, and Native American.
White colonialism led to the taking of land and power.
Conquer and destroy. White supremacy, so wrong.
Oh what a shame.
Great Spirit what is the lesson?
How long does the pain last?
The anger is gone. But my heart and soul still pain.
And my feelings hurt. Emotions high.
Why does racism still exist in the year 2000?
Ignorance still exists.
The inbred racism that passes from generation to generation still remains today and is prevalent.
The thought being whites are better than blacks.
Whites still step back intentionally to let blacks open the doors.
Mortgage companies, loan companies, home and apartment rentals still prefer white to black clients.
Huge apartment complexes always place blacks at the back of the complex due to loud music or loud talk, so whites say.
Where is the equality?
Oh how my heart and soul hurts.
Whites are employed before blacks.
My solar plexus is in a knot.
My child, surrender and release your burden.
Accept as is. Move forward.
Now is the moment of your power.
Educate and teach. Pray. Create prayer chains.
Keep your eye on the prize and hope alive.
The Rainbow Tribe Vision and The Whirling Rainbow Dance are still alive.
Be true to your authentic self.
Teach the lessons of your heart and soul.
Walk in balance and harmony.
Along The Sacred Path of Beauty,
many will join the tribe
and unity, equality, and wholeness,
will be alive and live on.

HO

CLEANSING

At this time
we are one with each other,
One with the Creator
fine-tuned to the flow and rhythm of Mother Earth.
Coming together
shedding much pain and anger.
Each layer releasing the toxins of the past
for a lighter, brighter me
A kind, forgiving, and compassionate me.
Cleansing,
A time to rid the past
A time for death and dying
A time for renewal and rebirth
A time of change and empowerment
A time to be grounded and rooted in Mother Earth.
This time made me feel her energy as she nurtured and re-energized my mind, body, and soul.
Mother Earth reconnects to Father Sky
for the oneness and Godliness of Self,
a great love -experience
of soul and Creator connection,
Cleansing,
good for the mind, body, and soul
A time to be whole.

HO

Searching Soul For Truth and Light

WHAT IS CHANGE?

What is change?
It is enrolling in unlimited possibilities.
Making choices
Changing your life
Releasing the past of old familiar ways
Living life through others
Fulfilling others' expectations of you.
Accepting self and others as is
helps one face fears and accept one's truth.
Truth with gentle words of kindness, compassion, and forgiveness,
letting go of inauthentic ways that have held you back,
back in a world that is uptight and serious.
Moving forward with your emotions,
accepting the truth of your heart and soul
brings forward one's authentic self.
To one who has begun the journey of self-healing
for transformation, self-empowerment, and freedom,
this newfound love,
changes a person into one of high positive energy
Willing to share the experience,
of integrity, authenticity, courage,
and unlimited possibilities
We can all be empowered and free.
Rid yourself of blockages, burdens, and challenges
Move forward
to the truth of your heart and soul
Great Spirit is always with you,
Loving you unconditionally
Feel this love and peace
and let your authentic self shine
to be whole and complete.

CREATIVE MIND

A creative soul
A beautiful spirit
that has taken steps
to remove some layers from her soul.
Experiencing the light within
Expressing her self
made her feel her soul.
As the Creator fills her spirit with love many
prayers have be said
That has left her respectful and humble.
        Now;
Prayers answered,
She is ready
to take the challenge of her spiritual journey
to move forward
along her soul path
Glowing
Radiating
Overjoyed with her answered prayers
her kind, gentle spirit
moves forward
Along her path
        Remembering:
The Creator, above all
One love;
Safe journey, maiden.

Marva Samuels

SERENITY

As I sit serenely in my Sacred Space,
Mount Shasta is calling.
It is calling for me to be healed, restored, harmonized, empowered, and free.
The serenity of the mountain
makes me feel calm, kind, compassionate, and loving
with a definite release of a brighter, lighter me.
The colors are green, pink, blue, yellow, and gold.
The river speaks loudly
of going with the flow.
Seen in the river's reflection
are the vibrant colors of pink and green,
making me feel safe in God's loving, sacred land.
My medicine wheel is awakened
and I sit in the West letting my visions flow.
Great Spirit, my faith and belief in You continues to grow,
making me love You more and more.
Deeper and deeper I go to the depths of my soul
gaining more wisdom as my spirit expands.
Surrendering all my burdens, as I am told,
for the time has come for me to open up and shift within
so my heavy heart can be released.
Tears, tears, tears to flow.
So let the river of tears flow.
The time is now
so,
let the river of tears flow.
So I can love again
Be myself
And feel my emotions rise.
Love myself from the depths within
So I can be the healer and teacher You have me to be.
With love, gratitude, honor, respect and prayer,
Great Spirit,
I surrender all.

HO

MY SPECIAL JOURNEY

My kundalini is running with blockages and challenges released.
Dedication, determination, and endurance have paid off.
Always remaining focused on being healed, empowered, and free.
Letting go of the blockages that maintained my bondage
released the power and control of my father
Oh, how the power of childhood trauma held me back.
It took strength and courage to move forward.
And see that I am fearless.
The journey was painful.
Returning to the past to face fears of trauma
helped me face it, engulf it, relive it, and release it.
Sometimes it controlled my every living moment;
anger, disgust, fear, sadness, and hatred surfaced to the maximum.
Oh what a heavy burden!
I cried. *God help me! God help me!*
I cried long and lonely nights
Finally, I began to use my spiritual tools.
Meditation, stillness, and silence made me listen to my voices.
Asking to face my Dad,
here, in a vision, I was reborn.
My Dad appeared and felt my power and strength.
Cowered in a corner with his hands and arms covering his head and
face, afraid to look at me, afraid I would beat him to death.
But in that special, precious, and loving moment
I felt his pain, sadness, and fear of his childhood trauma of molestation.
I cried tears of sadness for him, but tears of joy for me
No longer a victim, because at that moment
I forgave him then myself completely.
I voiced words I thought I would never say or mean.
"Daddy, I forgive you and I still love you."
The burden finally released.
I smiled and felt energy of joy vibrating throughout my body.
Empowered, healed, and free, walking in balance and harmony
I felt love, joy, peace, and happiness
With a new found energy of being whole and complete.
My kundalini running, all chakras spinning freely and glowing brightly,
My powered and strength restored
Love and forgiveness within and without
glowing radiantly in the light
I thanked Great Spirit
for my special journey
and for the lessons and blessings I received and yet to come.
I am abundant and full of love and joy,
Safe journey.

HO

A GIFT OF LOVE

I met a special lady
as beautiful as she can be
Full of love and kindness
Glowing radiantly
Talking, talking, talking
sharing what she knew
Words of gentle wisdom,
Acts of authentic beauty,
and emotions of pure delight
Her fingers soothed and unblocked my energy
Massaging my body gently, then firmly, released tension and stress
Created a change in energy
This change was our connection
to our soul-love and energy
I thanked Great Spirit for our paths connecting
because she gave me what I needed
Love and joy within
and a gift of love and kindness
With sisterly love
She placed her Indian sterile silver necklace around my neck
saying her spirit guides led her to do this
because this gift was mine, to be
A special give away
A gift of love, joy, and kindness
Now mine to wear radiantly and mine to give spiritually.

HO

ANCHOR

The Anchor,
Stability
An attachment to hold on to
Is it good or bad?
An Anchor,
Stability
to ground and center
to align with Great Spirit.
An Anchor,
not to be used and abused
So
Set the tone
Make your boundaries
Seek higher guidance
Listen to your inner voices
Because
Not every call is meant for you.

HO

MY HOME

My home is such a sacred place.
Full of love and joy,
peace and happiness;
a place of respect and honor,
providing the space I need.
A place of change and freedom,
stress- and tension-free,
a temple to honor Great Spirit
and connect to my spiritual energy.
A path of soul-love and soul-energy,
surrendering all my being
to the Holy God and Goddess above,
connecting my inner being
to the Oneness and Godliness of self.
Each and every day I meditate for my answers,
Knowing I'll be healed, restored, empowered, and free
living in peace, joy, and harmony
So I pray and worship Great Spirit
in my sacred temple,
letting my home glow serenely.

WALKING IN BALANCE AND HARMONY

I walk in balance and harmony.
I walk in balance and harmony.
I understand the warrior of my male side.
I understand the nurturing and loving nature of my female side.
Together, I walk the middle ground
In balance and harmony,
following the path of my Grandmothers,
the Ancient Ones,
Seeking the wisdom in the Elder's Council
understanding my growth and transformation comes from my leap of faith,
Showing respect, honor, and gratitude at all times.
Moving forward with confidence,
healing the scars,
developing my creativity
with Great Spirit by my side.
Sacredness and Ceremony,
I am determined and committed to my path.
I walk in balance and harmony.
I walk in balance and harmony.
Acceptance is as is.
I walk with Rainbow Medicine.
The love and joy within, equals the love and joy without.
Purity is impeccability.
And I am filled with truth, purity, equality, and wholeness.
I walk in balance and harmony.
I walk in balance and harmony.

HO

GOD ABOVE ALL

God is love.
God is purity.
God is the pure, white light.
God is divine truth.
God is King of the Universe.
Revealing all truths.
Because he is all knowing and loving,
Creating all things with love that exists with energy.
We all have the ability to seek a higher level.
So we must exhale the negative and inhale the positive.
Take time away from the problem.
Give burdens to God to handle.
Live on prayer and faith.
Know the laws of attraction.
Attention goes where energy flows.
The world is what you create.
So we must seek the Oneness and Godliness of Self.
To be rich in love, peace, joy, and happiness.

HO

Searching Soul For Truth and Light

IN THE SILENCE

Be Still.
Be Silent.
Let the energies flow within.
Search for the flicker of The Eternal Flame,
Let it glow and feel your rhythm
as your heart pulsates to the beat of the drum.
Relax and breathe.
Go deep within your heart and soul
Listen and hear the voices.
Can you hear them?
Relax and let your body flow
as it takes you up, above, and beyond;
Great Spirit is calling.
Let the Great Mystery and Void
connect with your inner spirit.
Open up your heart and soul.
Fear not of the darkness;
Let the blackness be a comfort to you.
See your soul emerge in the sparkling light of white and pink
Pulsating and glowing,
Sparkling like a diamond,
Surrounded by the color pink
Radiating love and purity
Feel the joy as your body flows in rhythm with Great Spirit:
Balance and Harmony
Love and Joy
Peace and Happiness
Life and Wisdom
Equality and Unity
We are all one people.
So, lets dance and celebrate,
the Whirling Rainbow Dance.

Sing, dance, drum, rattle, and chant!
Let yourself be free!
Feel Mother Earth,
as she caresses and nurtures you.
Let the energy flow,
and saturate each and every molecule of you body.
Let it spiral up, then down your chakras
cleansing you of all your impurities.
Surrender
as the heaviness of your burdens is released.
Feel the joy
as you become lighter and brighter
your aura and being surrounded by love.
The diamond is sparkling,
The sun is shining brilliantly,
The red rose has appeared.
My spiritual energy is glowing
in the color yellow!
Every where I look things are glowing yellow.
As I look up,
I see an angel with yellow wings
glowing in a white, sparkling gown.

But look!
There she stood,
dressed in a black hooded cloak
With a staff in her right hand
Grandmother She-Who-Listens.
Be Still.
Be Silent.
Hear The Truth.

Marva Samuels

TRUTH

Truth is honesty.
Truth is divine purity.
A love of the Oneness and Godliness of Self,
seeking spirit within to face fears
Fears of physical, mental, emotional, and spiritual burdens
that weigh heavy on our minds
and linger, feeding the ego with comfortable lies,
leaving one in a state of denial,
afraid to look directly in the mirror and face the shadows.
Yes, the shadows are still you.
It's strange how the negative makes one at ease with the dark.
But once the burden is lifted in the light,
one changes from being powerless to confident,
with a positive attitude.
With matters of truth and matters of the heart,
love and affection,
kindness and compassion,
fills the heart and soul.
Seeking inner truth sheds many tears.
Truth, honesty, and purity of self are easy to create
and a journey full of self-love
that once filled
can be shared with all of mankind.

HO

Marva Samuels

ABOVE AND BEYOND

Many times I wondered.
What it would be like.
To go Above and Beyond,
soaring like the Eagle
to great heights,
exploring the Universe,
feeling freedom and total bliss
understanding the joy and peace of the Master's
Unconditional Love.
The Goddess within and without glowing radiantly,
the little *me* finally stepping aside,
while the bigger me, comes forward
connects The Oneness and Godliness of Self.
Non-judgmental attitude,
acceptance of what is,
No matter what
And continuing to love
Radiating with beauty
Speaking with truth of the soul
with gentleness, kindness, compassion, and love.
Forgiveness of the utmost,
always positive,
letting the love shine
thankful to Great Spirit
for all of my lessons, and blessings, and
abundance and connection to,
Above and Beyond.

HO

SACRED MOUNTAIN

Mount Shasta, you beautiful , magnificent mountain,
Your spiritual presence brings serenity, peace, and joy.
And in your spiritual presence there is stillness
That brings answers from Great Spirit.
If one's intention was authentic, one's prayers were answered.
As we observed The Sky Nation, Creature Beings, Standing People,
We receive our messages.
We inhaled a deep breath and exhaled,
Breathing a breath of new life
Remembering to breathe, brings the jumping of the waves
With the opening and closing of energies,
This newfound energy brings joy and happiness.
Sometimes happiness is expressed with tears.
These tears are our cleansing medicine,
Helping us to release the pain, wounds, and scars of many years.
Wounded babies, we are.
Preparing for the time to release our pain from the depths of our heart and soul,
we waited in anticipation.
Cleansing with tears
Assisted us with sharing, caring, loving, and trusting each other
Challenges, at times, that seemed very difficult.
But the world is what you create
There are no limits.
So, Sacred Mountain, I thank you for my cleansing tears,
My honesty and truth in sacred circle,
Plus, my love of sisterhood.
But most of all,
I thank you for bringing my self-love to the surface,
Shredding another layer of pain,
Allowing me to be calm in the stillness,
To listen to my lessons and blessings.
And most of all
For giving me the answer
to go with the flow of the river.
Great Mountain I have learned; never fear one's tears of sadness
Because they are also one's tear's of joy.
Safe journey.

HO

NATURE'S BEAUTY

The park is a haven.
A place of pure delight;
Walks in nature's beauty
Provide such serenity.
A place of peace and quiet
From the world's insanity,
The energies of the birds, animal, insects, trees, stones, earth, and clouds
Surround my being.
The Keepers of the Four Wind and Direction
Accentuate the elements of earth, wind, air, and fire.
The vibrant colors of the plants, trees, grass, and earth
The soft breeze of the wind,
The warmth of the sun,
And the openness of the sky
Create inner peace.
Mother Earth and Father Sky assist with the change of energy.
With each and every deep breath
My mind, body, and soul begin to feel the energy flow.
Feeling that special presence of the fire and passion within,
I communicated with nature
For the answer I needed.
Finding peace and joy
In the silence
Calmed my nerves,
Great Spirit,
Filled my heart and soul
With nature's natural beauty,
Caressed and nurtured me with His presence,
I felt the Oneness and Godliness of Self within
And I took time again
To thank Him
For nature's natural beauty.

HO

EARTH HEALING

As we surround the tree in a circle,
A sacred space is created with smudge, light, prayer, and love.
Holding hands gathers and combines energy as one.
Such a rich and rewarding feeling
as we center ourselves in prayer.
we give thanks, honor, and gratitude to Great Spirit, Mother Earth, Father Sky, Keepers of the Four Winds and the Four Directions, and all of the Ancestors that have passed before us.
We call on the dolphin, the sacred breath of life.
Combining our energies as one,
we ask Great Spirit for love and peace of all mankind,
with a pure, white light in our prayers
feeling the peace, joy, and harmony.
Mother Earth and Father Sky are always present.
Great Spirit is telling us loud and clear
that meditation with intention for the love of all is needed.
And the time
Is now.

HO

SUMMER DAY

Clear blue skies
Warm breezes
Bright radiant sun
Oh, what a beautiful summer day.
Flowers in blossom
Bright vibrant colors
Green, healthy grass
Mother Earth vibrating joy and love
Father Sky vibrating change and freedom
Birds singing songs of happiness
Wind blowing freely
Water flowing in rhythm with the life forces
Earth creating that grounding spirit
Fire creating the passion of the soul within.
A day of rejoicing,
Thanking Great Spirit for all of the creation.
Thankful for all that is received and not received.
Great Spirit understands the needs of everything and everyone.
So, from all of the universe,
we thank you Great Spirit,
for a beautiful summer day.

HO

THE REDWOOD TREES

Redwood trees so tall and massive, vibrating new life-
energy connecting my soul energy, creating love-energy
of peace, joy, balance, and harmony.
Serenity and tranquility,
Great Spirit's natural beauty,
lifting me higher, and higher, and higher,
filling my mind, body, and soul with joy to the highest degree.
Awakening my spirit,
cleansing my chakras,
and running my kundalini,
The Godliness of Self energizing,
As one with The Goddess and Mother Earth,
glowing radiantly pure, white and green light,
peace and serenity,
Oh, what a joy.
Great Spirit is calling.
Return to Mother Earth
for her grounding and nurturing Spirit.
Feel Her energy vibrate
while your energy comes alive.
Hug, caress, and love the earth.
Listen.
Be still.
Hear the voices
come alive like me.
Transform and share your beauty.
Like The Redwood Trees.

HO

Searching Soul For Truth and Light

MEDICINE MAN

Medicine Man,
Who are you?
I am the healer and teacher of the tribe.
I heal the mind, body, and soul.
I make one whole on all planes
mentally, physically, emotionally, and spiritually.
Visions and dreams assist with
bringing the blockage and challenges forward into the present.
Sweat lodge detoxifies, then purifies your mind, body, and soul.
Cleansing and releasing the toxins,
while chanting, praying, singing, and drumming helps connect our soul
to Father Sky and Mother Earth.
Here I pray that Great Spirit will assist me in the healing
changing negative energy to positive energy.
Great Spirit, the masters, totems, and spirit guides will assist me,
and give me the answers and methods of healing.
Instruction to be done exactly as presented
so the healing can be successful.
I draw my powers from Great Spirit and The Universe.
Our soul connection keeps my heart and soul pure,
and full with the pure, white light
glowing radiantly.
Plus, I teach rituals, ceremonies, and my craft to others,
only teaching those who have been sent by Great Spirit.
The initiation can be rough
enduring years of apprenticeship,
but the journey within and beyond are rewarding.
Understanding self-empowerment leads to service of mankind.
Going within,
connecting with Great Spirit
creates magic.
And this magic is power.
Not to be abused.
That is why the Medicine Man is the healer and teacher of the tribe.

MOTHER EARTH

The land is the Universal Home
So that all can live together in unity
There is balance and harmony with the land.
Mother Earth is a nurturing, loving, and grounding Spirit.
When all is healthy,
Mother Earth is the color of vibrant green.
The earth is rich with red or black soil.
Here the grass and trees grow lushly.
In the valleys, plains, hills, and mountains
Mother Earth radiates love,
Letting the seeds of plants and trees grow abundantly.
The richness of the soil feeds Mother Earth providing healthy nourishment.
That allows Her to vibrate healthy energy,
and pulsate strongly to the beat of the drum.
This environment provides serenity,
Love and joy,
Peace and happiness,
Balance and harmony,
Silence and laughter,
Stillness and movement
Of all things.
Take time,
Feel the rhythm of Mother Earth. Connect with her vibration.
Flow in unison.
Open up to receive the love of Mother Earth
Allowing the healing.
Feel the cleansing of your chakras
Let the energy spiral and feel the rise of your kundalini.
Go deep
Within Mother Earth.
Feel Her warm, loving caress as your body tingles all over,
releasing the heaviness of your burdens.
Open up,
Receive the warmth and love of Mother Earth.
Ground your spirit. Connect with your heart and soul,
And glow radiantly
With the nurturing loving spirit of Mother Earth.

HO

DEER HEART

LONG DANCE

Ceremony, ceremony, ceremony,
Let's all celebrate.
Women of all races, colors, and creeds together as one in unity
Solidarity of sisterhood
No matter where you are from, what color you are
or what sisterhood you are from.
Unity of sisterhood
for the common cause of praying, dancing, and singing together
for the burdens of women and children of today and generations to come
Great Spirit joins us as we give thanks for our abundance and kindness.
As we give thanks from our soul,
within we rejoice.
From dust 'till dawn we sing, dance, and drum in a circular motion
Keeping our energies high for the common cause of pain, abuse, and fear
Women and children have had to carry.
Here, women in the privacy of a Sacred Circle,
express their truth, love, and emotions
for the highest good of all.
For peace, enlightenment, clarity, healing,
empowerment and freedom,
as we honor our Elders, Ancestors, Keepers of the Four Winds
and Keepers of the Four Directions, All of our Relations.
We dance the Whirling Rainbow Dance
for unity and wholeness.
Purification of soul
Prayer and inner peace.
Love, joy, peace, and happiness for all
for the pain, abuse, and burdens of women and children
for the healing of Mother Earth
and the unity of sisterhood.
Tired, worn out, and fatigued energy elevates for sunrise.
Here we dance, sing, drum, chant, and howl
as we give prayer and deliverance,
honor and gratitude.
and dance the Victory Dance
to All Our Relations.

HO

PURIFICATION

Purification, set me free.
Cleanse me of my impurities.
Take the key,
unlock the door,
open it up and set me free.
Release the burdens throughout my years
those first of longevity.
Cleanse my mind, body, and soul
Make my heart and soul sweat heavy
for years of negativity,
giving up all my burdens and pain
cleansing my soul,
surrendering all.
Great Spirit, cleanse all of my impurities.
Making a lighter and brighter me,
a loving and caring being
with a pure light of divinity.
Joy and happiness,
Peace and harmony,
Kindness and compassion,
cleanse me of my impurities.
My authentic self is crying to be free.
Make me the woman I am to be;
Great Spirit set me free.
Cleanse me of my impurities.

APOPHYLITE

Apophylite, what a beautiful stone you are
white and green crystal.
I place you gently in my left hand
and feel your energy.
With the calling of a red candle
I go within my heart and soul
and meditate on your energy.
Here I see the yellow and black butterfly with the green grasshopper,
telling me to look for changes with great leaps
What a joy you bring.
Smiling with joy,
I venture forward seeing the black then white horse
in the glow of red and yellow.
Here I thank Great Spirit,
for my acceptance of The Void and my spiritual awakening.
Knowing and understanding
my journey will bring expansion, travel, power, and freedom.
Aligning my male and female energies in balance and harmony
slowly, my divine soul of yellow rimmed with red
surrounded in the blue cross
connected with my soul-love of yellow glowing in a white border.
That spiritual awakening filled me with complete energy.
Awakening my kundalini was a power surge
starting with spiraling energy at my feet
moving up my legs, connecting with each and every chakra,
releasing all my blockages.
As my kundalini rose from chakra to chakra, I took a deep breath
which felt like the breath of a newborn baby.
Rebirth with each new breath brought on emotions of joy.
I began to hear the voices:
Learn the truth,
Be the truth,
Speak the truth,
Honor the truth.
Here I felt my spiritual and emotional connection.
This lightness awakened my being and heart chakra.
Oh apophylite, what a beautiful stone you are,
full of unconditional love and joyful glee.

HO

THE LIGHT

My kundalini is running.
My chakras are all lit up.
Energy is alive.
Running,
Pulsating,
Flowing,
Glowing,
Radiating,
I shine.
My soul is connecting
in unity with the Goddess Head
here in the moment,
unconditional love beams from every atom of my body.
My body is warm and tingling all over.
Filling with the life forces of
Love and happiness
Peace and joy;
and, most importantly,
filling with the Golden Sun,
Radiance, protection, and purity.
The power from within
gives illumination, clarity, and understanding.
Purity of the soul,
with detachment and loving energy, always
gives rebirth of the authentic self.
Truth, honor, respect, and gratitude are the keys
to discovery, transformation, and empowerment.
Returning to the Source,
Great Spirit,
Pulsating to the rhythm of Mother Earth
Soaring above and beyond to Father Sky
brings reverence of the soul.
Glowing within and without
my aura creating my sacred space.
As I glow radiantly,
I feel my healing powers,
in the brilliance of The Light.

HO

THE SUN

Brightly he shines up above
giving warmth and heat to all things.
Vibrating energy
of strength, power, and healing.
The Sun
provides healing,
allows all in the universe to grow,
to grow and mature on their journey.
He is the supreme cosmic energy
giving heat and light,
Illuminating the Skies,
heating the Universe.
He gives sunshine.
Life and death,
with the rising and setting of the Sun
Healing,
New beginnings,
Energy,
Strength,
and Power.
Look to the Sun.
and let the healing energy penetrate your mind, body, and soul
Let the white, radiant light pulsate and glow
into a blue purple aura
surrounded with a gold border.
It pulsates and heals,
and sends blue, healing balls
to all in need,
Open up.
Receive your blue ball
of illumination, strength, power, and intuitive knowledge,
for a healing from:
The Sun.

FULL MOON

Full moon
what a beautiful moon you are.
Shining brightly,
Radiating brilliance,
Pulsating strength and power;
my energy is high.
My intention for the good of all,
the time is right.
Goals are completed.
New commitments made.
Awareness expanding
Illumination of plans and goals,
Dreams becoming realities;
Spirit is surging with energy.
How brightly you shine,
In the darkness of the night
the color blue surrounds your presence,
and your aura
is pulsating the color blue.
I feel your strength and power.
My body is electrified with your energy.
Excitement fills my every cell.
As I begin to feel the calmness, peace, joy, and
happiness that your nurturing spirit brings,
I align with the rhythm of my feminine powers
and feel my strength.
Understanding my blessings,
and thankful for my abundance,
knowing I can soar to great heights
The possibilities unlimited,
deepening my trust and faith in Great Spirit.

HO

I WEEP

I weep, I weep, I weep
for the war created.
I weep
For souls lost
and the increasing death toll
Families lost and destroyed
Love lost
I weep.
Destruction
Devastation
Destroyer
Human suffering
I weep.
Slow response
to Katrina for the poor
Black or white
but predominantly black
Let many see
our leadership
of lost human spirit
Cold and non-caring
for those less fortunate than themselves.
I weep, I weep, I weep.
With such disrespect
our government moved forward with lights dim
I weep.
For those left behind
Life unfolded with despair
I weep, I weep, I weep
Equality and justice
Justice and unity
Where do we stand?
Is it that hard to care for another?
Do power and greed erase the human spirit?
Has our government lost that caring feeling?
Where do we go?

Who do we turn to?
Who is responsible?
Does the government really care?
I weep.
CREATOR
I beg
for your light of love and understanding
for your light of caring and sharing.
Shine it on our souls
fill our hearts
with love, peace, joy, and happiness
as we learn our truth
to love and care for another
to help one another
no matter what.
For the grace of Great Spirit
I continue to lift my hands in prayer
to connect our spirits
and feel the love.
You Are.
Hoping and praying
Lessons will take hold
Leadership, our example
Truth be told
Tells the story
of one lost soul
I weep
I weep
I weep
But
I wait with understanding
that the Creator will conquer all
Until then
I continue with my giving heart
and weep.

HO

HAITI

Haiti! Haiti!
For the love of God
Stop the shaking, Stop the shaking.
As the earthquake vibrated and shook the earth
Fear reigned.
Alive and living,
Fear reigned.
Destroying all in its path;
people, buildings, homes crumbled to the ground.
As Haiti shook, devastation soared.
Crumbling buildings to the ground,
Killing many people, adults and children
No matter the race, creed, or religion
Nothing spared; all equal in the eyes of God.
Immediate death for some, slow death for others,
Some lucky to be alive
Areas hit hard, some barely touched
Devastation, devastation, devastation.
In this moment of despair,
GOD ABOVE ALL
Kept the Haitian spirit alive;
People helping people,
Digging through the rubble to help save lives
Be the person known or unknown.
Covering the dead with sheets for respect and dignity.
Expressed human kindness, compassion, and love of one another
Sparked the life of Haiti and the Haitian people.
Crying for help, their voices were heard around the world.
The Red Cross, Presidents, celebrities, and ordinary people answered the call. Help was on the way
Human hearts and souls rose to the occasion
Letting us all know, letting us all know,
We are one
and we can work together for the common good of all mankind.
Love one another as you love yourself.
GOD ABOVE ALL
The Haitian spirit never dies.   Haiti is still alive.
Haiti! Haiti!
For the love of God.

JOURNEY

As one sheds layer after layer of emotional turmoil, the journey on one's path of self-awaken, self-discovery, self-transformation and self-empowerment begins.

Here, one cries out for the soul to direct and guide self with lessons, blessings, and abundance on the journey of Truth and Light.

THE BEGINNING

Who are you?
I am a Warrior
with a large feather headdress flowing down my back.
I represent strength, courage, wisdom, leadership, responsibility, and control.
The world has my aura so strong
I am left untouched.
Inner self is calling.
Am I really listening?
I soar with the eagle to Father Sky
to reach the heights of The Void and Great Spirit.
I land on a mountain cliff
overlooking the plains and meadows
to feel Mother Earth and her grounding Spirit.
In the silence I hear Great Spirit
telling me what I need to know.
Voices are calm, soft, and clear.
Be calm,
Be Patient,
Be Loving
Slow Down,
Be Balanced.
Great Spirit is calling.
Am I Ready?
Safe journey.

HO

AWAKENING

Do you see the sparkling white light?
Yes.
Right, left, up, down, above, below, and all around,
Everywhere I go.
What is it?
I can't shake it loose.
Don't be afraid.
Let your inner being awaken.
Remember it's been dormant a long time.
Feel the energy pulsate.
Let it flow.
Great Spirit is calling.
Are you ready to ride?

HO

THE CALLING

Something is calling.
I can't shake it.
It's penetrating to my soul.
My heart is opening up.
What is it?
Can you tell me?
My essence is being lifted up.
My whole being feels a surge of energy.
Who can I tell?
Where is the whale?
Sing to me,
I'm listening.
Remind me of times of old.
Precious, Precious, Precious times of old.
Truth is the answer I seek.
Dolphin, the common communicator of sound and rhythm,
Sacred Breath of Life
I need.
The waves are calling.
Are you ready to ride?
Emotions are high.
Great Spirit has all the answers.
Eagle your spirit soars to the Great Divine.
Lessons and blessings are near,
Soar like the eagle.
Gather your courage.
and feel
The Calling of The Void.

HO

Marva Samuels

DECISIONS

The feeling is back, and I feel strange.
My inner energy is increasing and decreasing
in ways that catch my attention
and make me feel the situation.
My mind is saturated.
Something inside is telling me it's time.
I feel my inner breath slow down and my inner energies calm.
That fear returns with the opening up of new energies and voices.
Great Spirit, protect me from negative energy.
Curiosity is high.
The Void keeps calling. *Do it. The time is right.*
More visions, less thought, more emotions;
the teacher and classes are present.
Apprenticeship is surrounding my aura.
That feeling of knowing, not knowing, but knowing is energizing?
I look at my Shaman Teacher and say, "Is she a pure medicine teacher?"
The feeling is so strong this time.
Purity, positivity, peace, tranquility, love, and wisdom surround the medicine teacher
The light is white, and my color is green.
My heart is beating to the sound of the drums.
The rhythm is natural, a feeling of long ago.
My spirit is calling.
My mind remembers those ugly times
of the negative spirit snatching my powers in the night.
The dark side is not for me.
Great Spirit protect me with a pure, white light.
I look at my teacher and say, " It's her. She will teach me."
Knowing but not knowing is vibrating.
A feeling of strength and power;
I can't shake it now. The energy is alive.
My feelings are changing. I'm calm, happy, excited, and fearful.
Meditation gives me my answer.
It's time. The call is made. No turning back.
The direction of my path has changed and my soul returns.
I lift my arms to Great Spirit in prayer.
Safe journey, maiden.

HO

BURDENS LIFTED

Many burdens
make our hearts heavy
bringing on negative feelings,
leaving us in disarray,
energies unbalanced.
With inner- and outer-being in turmoil,
unhappy souls are created.
Lift up your burdens to Great Spirits,
give prayer and thanks;
with intention let Great Spirit change your energy
let the white light fill your heart and soul,
and realize the journey is not easy.
With many challenges to conquer,
remember, maidens,
positive energy is the best.
Use your tools of knowledge
to maintain peace, balance, and harmony,
and maidens, your burdens will be lifted.

HO

TO MY TRUTH

As I stand alone in the valley surrounded by mountains,
with the river flowing in the West, I reflect back on my spiritual journey of knowing, not knowing, but knowing
Searching for that spiritual light that would open up my heart chakras;
my solar plexus was crying to be healed and free.
Somehow my mind with thoughts, words, and deeds,
was carrying heavy burdens of my short lifetime.
Burdens of abuse, victimization, shame, guilt, fears, aloneness,
and lack of self-love surfaced.
I cried for a softer, lighter, and brighter me.
I prayed to Great Spirit for a new beginning.
And I knew my prayers would be answered due to faith and belief in Him.
Great Spirit was the answer.
He was the light, truth, and guidance.
My prayer was answered.
I joined a Native American Spiritual group
that has given me a new breath of life,
opening my solar plexus and heart chakras,
made me answer The Call of The Void.
Here in the Great Mystery,
I began to understand my woman's intuition
and accept my visions and dreams.
I began to listen to the voices.
The voices were loud and clear.
"Be still. Be silent. Be Calm. I am here to guide you along your journey.
My words will be your wisdom. Let your intentions be of love, joy, peace,
and harmony that will benefit you, your environment, and your nation." As
I progressed, I began to see the connection and importance
between women's medicine, women power and women moon time
Accepting the responsibility of creation, imagination and creativity,
and love of the young.
Women give birth and keep the inner child alive by expressing truth,
creating inner joy,
and sharing wisdom of understanding, compassion, kindness, forgiveness
self-nurturing, and self-love;

all of these things bring forth the importance of women's group. Here in the Sacred Circle we bond together in sisterhood, making a group sanctuary of love and understanding.
But we must remember,
to fly like the eagle, raven, and crow,
and accept the reason why we are together
and ask ourselves, " Is this union for a season or a lifetime?"
And if it is for a season,
hug and kiss your sister
and send her on her way with love and prayer,
and the guidance of Great Spirit.
There are many sisterhoods
and hopefully, she will find her home.
As we walk our path,
The Sacred Laws never change.
Sacred Laws are the truth.
So, Sweet Maiden,
to your truth,
it will heal, restore, empower, harmonize and set you free.
Safe journey, Maiden.

HO

1998

The Beginning…
Recognizing that the warrior or male side of me was too dominate
and leading with negative energy,
A need for balance surfaced.
Letting the female side rise up and seek the qualities of a kind,
gentle, calm, peaceful, and loving being.
The awakening of the feminine side brought feelings of a deeper emotional spirit
that led to, "The Calling of the Void".
This calling has awakened my spirit, which has manifested into the flame of light within.
My heart beats in unison with the rhythm of the drum.
No longer afraid to go within my heart chakra and feel the Oneness and Godliness of Self
for a feeling of peace, tranquility, and happiness,
Exploring my inner being with meditation has heightened my ability,
to see visions, remember dreams, and hear and feel the voices with understanding.
My change of direction has also opened up my creative abilities.
This year has been a year of abundance, even with the stress of the world.
The Dolphin has given me the breath of life I need,
through the communication of sound and rhythm.
The Whale has led me to call the ancient records,
and helped me make my decision regarding my spirituality.
The Raven has opened my heart and soul to
The Great Mystery and The Void to discover my magic.
The Eagle has taught me to soar to heights of Great Spirit and Father Sky,
spread my wings and feel freedom, peace, joy, and happiness.
Plus, perch on an oak limb and feel the grounding spirit of Mother Earth
as she nurtures me in her loving arms.
The Crow has taught me the sacred laws and to speak my inner truth.
As I reflect back on this year of 1998, I understand the medicine of the Wolf,
the pathfinder, who returns to the clan to teach and share.
The Millennium is here.
The Sisterhood must remain strong, solid, and loyal because the teachings must be known.
And now at the end of 1998,
with the releasing of My Death Arrow and the empowerment of My Act of Power,
I stand in the opened plain with the clear blue river in the background,
alone, surrounded by teepees with purple tassel toppings and purple borders to their opening,
And howl and sing the teaching of The Wolf.

HO

JANUARY 1999

Great Spirit, this is the year of the millennium.
The year women are to rediscover and reclaim their power
and lose that feeling of being victimized,
so the feminine side can give to the world without ego or selfishness.
Lessons taught will be of a Spiritual nature from within,
giving one a loving feeling of self and others,
with a kinder, deeper, sense of helping each other.
This is a time to seek the lighted flame within
where the worldly cares cannot intrude
so that we may rejoice in Great Spirit
and feel the peace, joy, and happiness of His love.
This is your connection to Great Spirit on your journey
so that the feminine side of a loving nurturing self
can unite with the masculine side of an aggressive, ego-centered warrior.
This bonding of marriage of male and female
will be a lasting bond within and without,
above and below, creating a strength and power never felt.
The glow of unity will be a pure, white light surrounded with a yellow border
with rays of white, blue, and purple.
Wise Women we will be
guided by the light of the Oneness and Godliness of Self within,
sharing all our knowledge and wisdom
to help deliver and create the Rainbow Tribe Vision into a reality.
And to bond with Sisterhood
so that we can love one another
no matter what race, religion, or creed.

HO

DEATH ARROW 1999

My medicine wheel made.
I smudged to cleanse the energy.
I rattled my wheel awake.
I offered my corn, tobacco, and prayers of gratitude.
I honored Great Spirit, Mother Earth, Father Sky, Grandmother Moon,
and Grandfather Sun, Keepers of the Four Winds and The Four Directions and All Our Ancestors.
I lit my candle and my intentions were made in prayer.
"Great Spirit, be present with me today and hear and feel my prayers."
As I cast away the year's challenges, burdens, and blockages,
I asked Great Spirit,
to make me whole, healed, fully restored, empowered, harmonized and free.
Help me, Goddess, see a lighter brighter me.
As I lit my bundle, I released my burdens, fears, and negativities of the year.
My vision clear, with the sun shining like a crystal diamond
sparkling with a yellow border
the colors of red, blue, green, pink, white, and yellow appeared.
The humming bird vibrating pure joy;
There she stood, firm and tall,
Cloaked in a black-hooded robe with a staff,
Grandmother, She-Who-Listens.
The message was clear, in the Silence and Stillness.
"Listen to your heart and soul
Hear the truth.
Awaken to the new you,
Transformed and lighter.
This is your peace, joy, love, and harmony.
Feel the union and connection of your body, soul, and spirit."
As I began to flow in rhythm with nature
I felt Mother Earth caress and nurture my body.
The duck, swan, pelican, and parrot appeared
filling me with emotions: faith, trust, innocence, lightness, buoyancy, and healing.
Suddenly, I felt complete heaviness through my entire body,
my hands cupped together, as my head fell into the palms of my hands,
the year's burdens, a heavy toll.
Slowly, my hands lifted up off my face and raised up in prayer and deliverance Thanking Goddess for Her lessons and blessings,
Death and Rebirth, Growth and Healing, my spiritual energy released, the color yellow,
Death completed.
Rebirth, and a new beginning on the horizon,
I journeyed forward.
Safe journey, maiden.

BEYOND THE SHADOWS

My, my, my
Am I really seeing the light?
Through the wounds of sadness, despair, neglect, abuse, poverty,
uselessness, aloneness, hopelessness, and nothingness
I finally see some light.
The tears of anger, pain, depression, despair, sorrow, and grief
are cleansing my heart and soul;
each level sheds another layer to bring a deeper feeling of self-love.
Somewhere in this cleansing of the tears, sadness, and wounds,
changes occurred that brought joy and happiness.
It was a time of peace and calmness, an incredible feeling of total bliss.
Oh, how awesome was this feeling.
Is this how heaven feels?
I soared to great heights with such serenity
while The Great Mystery and The Call of The Void
captured my complete being;
my aura was passionately aglow with a pure, white light.
I felt Great Spirit within my soul and heard,
"Love unconditionally, my child. You are here to serve as a teacher and healer.
I will always be at your side to guide you. It's time. Loving you always."
The words were so distinct.
Who was it?
Was it He?
He who? He who?
You know whom.
God, you are so funny.
You make me realize that laughter is such a joy of life.
Great Spirit, I have great faith and belief in you.
As I reflect back on my life since March '98
I am thankful for my lessons and blessings.
My growth was definitely seeking the root of my medicine,
Love, kindness, and gentleness
and my message was:
Maiden, await patiently,
Beyond the shadows,
For the Calling of the Angels.

HO

RELEASING THE CHAINS

I feel the tightness of my chest, hands, and feet.
Invisible chains have my hands and feet tied together;
these chains make me feel heavy burdens more profoundly.
Fatigue, decreased energy, increased stress, weight gain, water retention
and lack of strength filter through my body.
Something is just not right!
What is it? Can you help me?
Coyote season has surfaced my fears, fears I need to face
to regain my power and strength.
White versus black,
White magic versus black magic
Heterosexual versus homosexual
Group versus individual
Sisterhood versus aloneness
Financial stability versus broke
Oneness and Godliness of Self versus ego
these fears are my challenges.
Once dissected and nurtured, my fears will be released
and truth will be known. Truth will set me free,
bringing healing, empowerment, harmony, balance, freedom
and, most of all, self-love.
That self-approval is desperately needed to set me free
to soar like the eagle to Father Sky and The Great Mystery.
Chains of bondage shall be released
cleansing my aura, charkas, and body.
No one can step in my way and use me through channeling
because my truth will be my healing,
releasing the chains. No longer in bondage,
I will cry from the highest mountain:
"Free at last! Free at last!"
Freedom, freedom, freedom hear my soul cry.
As I feel Mother Earth caressing me in her arms
and nurturing me in my new found discovery,
The Oneness and Godliness of Self.
I lift my arms to Great Spirit in deliverance and prayer
thanking Him for always being there guiding and protecting me
then I dance and sing in love, peace, joy, happiness, and harmony
because I'm free.

HO

Searching Soul For Truth and Light

EVOLUTION DAY

My Evolution Day, a day of love, joy, peace, and happiness
a time of gathering and sharing
flowing with the energy of the heart and soul.
This time,
A Change,
Slow down. Be still. Listen.
The inner voices are speaking. Go within your heart and soul,
introspection-time is here.
Go deep
feel your energy shift
fast pace to slow-pace,
A time of reflection, letting go of the past and moving forward
transformation occurring.
Death and rebirth.
Feel the change.
I'm heavy, tired, and exhausted with little energy
Slow down. Be still. Listen.
This time,
A Change,
In soul and spiritual energy
letting my mind, body, soul, and spirit open up to my new energy.
Transformation,
My body and soul connecting preparing me for my spiritual journey,
A Journey,
Of soul-love and soul-energy
Going deeper and deeper into my soul
Feeling my cells explode within with joy,
Self-Love,
Being authentic, Real.
I lift my arms up to Great Spirit, In prayer and thanks,
expressing my gratitude for my lessons, blessings, and abundance
Knowing and understanding my evolution gift.
A Gift,
A gift of transformation,
of soul-love and love-energy,
a connection to the Goddess Head.
My Evolution Day.
Happy Evolution Day.

HO

SEXUAL ABUSE

How did it happen?
Why did it happen?
I'll never know now that my Dad is dead.
But it really happened.
Sexual abuse of a child is a sin greater than all,
especially when a parent abuses their child or children.
In my case, my dad.
It all started in fun with my youngest brothers and myself.
Wrestling with each other as we rolled on the floor and laughed.
Then suddenly I felt my self being molested by my dad.
As I kicked and screamed at my dad,
I felt surprised, confused, pain, rage, and betrayal.
This was wrong and not happening to me.
All I could do was kick at my Dad and scream;
his response was a smile, then laughter.
This seemed to excite him.
What a sick individual!
Dads do not harm their children.
I guess my dad was not a complete man,
Just a male with many problems and living a lie.
Effectiveness is the measurement of truth.
Dad, you did not make the grade.
So now at the age of 46, I'm still alone and not married.
Feeling a lack of trust in men,
lack of confidence and self-esteem,
with a loss of innocence, playfulness, respect, peace, joy, happiness, balance, and love of self.
It took me time.
But now I honor myself
because of the courage and strength I have to heal.
So I may feel love, happiness, peace, joy, harmony, and balance again.
Great Spirit states, this is mine to reclaim and be whole again.

HO

MY PRECIOUS BABY

I'm sorry I was not there for you,
but I'm here for you now.
I was out of the house at your time of need.
I tell you now
that you will never face that danger of betrayal again
that lost of trust, purity, and innocence
I'm here, Sweet pea,
to protect you forever.
I will always love you.
So now it is time to trust, to play, to be free, and to be innocent again.
Yes, the blame is no longer yours
but your Dad's.
He is the sexual abuser of a child,
And that child is you.
No longer alive, he is dead,
no longer able to touch you up close or at a distance.
The fears of being alone with him no longer exist
because I am here to protect you always.
So run, play, laugh, giggle, and be happy
Because you are finally free.

WHAT TIME IS IT?

What time is it?
It's time to heal.
A time of self-discovery, self-healing, and self-transformation.
Can I really heal?
Do I have the strength to look in the mirror and overcome
that fear of looking right in my eyes
and seeing where my emotions, my physical, my mental, and my spiritual scars are?
Can I do it?
Will I do it?
Child, to heal, you need faith, trust, and belief in Great Spirit.
Where is your faith?
Go deep within your heart and soul
to reach the Oneness and Godliness of Self,
visualize and light the flame within.
Go to the source,
listen to the voices
as they calmly speak
and tell you what you need to know.
Be Still.
Be Silent.
Be Strong.
Do not fear the voices.
Stand firm
and have courage to be strong.
Listen,
Feel the kindness, compassion, joy, happiness, peace, and love of the heart.
Surrender your being totally to Great Spirit,
who will show you your deepest hopes and dreams
and guide you along the way.
On your journey
fear is negative and useless.
It stops one from being able, healed, and free.
So ask yourself,
What time is it?
Child, it is time to heal.

HO

LOVE IS ALL I NEED

Love is all I need.
The sensation of warmth and tingling all over my body
Inside and outside,
The Glow:
A glow of the pure, white light
that ignites the flame within
the soul, heart, and crown connection
the Oneness and Godliness of Self.
Glowing in radiance of joy,
feeling the fluttering then pounding of my heart,
the passion of love growing within.
Love is all I need.
Love, the ingredient to surrender all to Great Spirit
The Glow:
God Above All.
Faith and belief in Great Spirit
gives that love and joy I need
that feeling of warmth, peace, joy, and harmony,
The Glow:
Is
All The Love I need.

SOUL WITHIN

Sitting here quietly
my mind wanders dreamily of you.
Only a few days have passed
since I last heard from you.
My inner flame glows luminously,
meditation bringing us closer
uniting us as one.
Physically, you are close to my heart.
Your warm voice, gentle touch, and warm glow lingers
forever on my mind and in my heart.
My thoughts travel peacefully with love and joy.
As I travel deeper and deeper into the Void
a vivid picture of our world is created.
Love, peace, joy, and happiness
surrounds and engulfs us
helping us meet our tasks of successes and failures.
Nothing stops us from proceeding
Inner-strength, determination; and we will find our way
I miss and love you
My inner-child
My inner-children
Your presence is always with me
Because all of me is you
And all of you are me
        Together
        We Are
        I AM.

HO

LOVING SELF

Balance of male and female energies, takes strength and love of self to reach.
Seeking that self-healing and self-transformation brings one freedom
yet taking on that first step brings fear, negativity, and depression.
Looking at self, seeing that aggressive warrior
Makes one realize you are in the depths of hell.

At that moment, one realizes it is time to change
The mind, especially the ego, makes it difficult to release wounds,
but once that decision is made, life becomes lighter and brighter.

Preparation begins with:
Going within to the depths of your heart and soul
Finding the burdens of your inner child
Facing your shadows and fear.
Releasing your burdens and negative energy for a softer you
Releasing the aggressive warrior for a softer, assertive warrior
with the feminine energies of a loving and nurturing maiden
Makes one whole with acceptance of self
The emotions are high and begin to flow.
I AM APPROVED.
I AM LOVE.

Life is full of joy, peace, and happiness
Loving self and helping one's inner child regains power,
making a loving bond.
That bond brings new beginnings with a new breath of life,
uniting male and female energies in marriage
with the colors of red, pink, and green, and the symbol of a red heart with a green border,
pulsating to the beat of the drum.
Power and strength restored balance and harmony of male and female energies
Life forces of:
Love and Joy
Peace and Happiness
I smile, dance, sing, drum, and pray
because Great Spirit has heard my prayers making me able and setting me free
finally,
into that beautiful pink rose.

HO

Searching Soul For Truth and Light

DO IT NOW

Do it.
Do it.
Do it now.
It's the time.
So do it now.
Gather all the tools, totems, and
information prepare yourself with what you
need venture out.
And do it now.
Make your wheel and find your spot
go deep within your sacred spot
Hear and see the answers flow
letting you feel what you need to know.
Listen.
Be calm.
Relax your body.
Because now it's time
to hear your heart and soul.
Speak to me.
Speak to me.
Tell me what I need to know.
Write and create what needs to be told.
Sing and dance rhythms of old.
Do it.
Do it.
Do it now.
Ha-Ha, Ha-Ha, Ha-Ha-Ha.

HO

Searching Soul For Truth and Light

SOUL RETRIEVAL

Excitement flowed.
With vibrating high energy through out my body
I lay on the floor in deep meditation
and I found myself in the Kiva.
Surrounded by large standing people.
Trees 50 to 60 feet tall
with branches slowly crossing over at the top,
creating a bridge,
that opened up to the pure, white light.
Here I released
the burdens and challenges of the past and present.
And opened up my heart to the love of the pure, white light.
Deeper and deeper I ventured into the dream world,
with the eagle, swan, bear, black panther, and wolf to guide me.
As each animal appeared
the angel glowed in the colors of pink and white.
I felt safe and secure.
trusting and believing in Great Spirit,
surrendering myself to the unknown,
I felt sheltered and protected.
Symbols appeared.
The wedding band, diamond marquis, five-pointed star, large single diamond, and rose,
created energy of union, power, strength, life, and death and rebirth.
Soul Retrieval.
A healing with a great sense of freedom.
As each soul was blown back into my heart then crown chakra,
I felt warmth and love.
To each soul part returned
I stated,
Welcome Home.
And now, the journey begins.

HO

SOUL-LOVE

I feel my soul awakening.
lighting up my mind, body, and soul
each and every molecule
vibrating in the light,
warmth of love
and the tingling of energy
caressing my body.
Light energy
flows into my crown chakra
and spirals down my center
radiating out from the heart
creating my Sacred Temple.
It is the Divine Light
and the Upper World I seek.
The home of The Enlightened Ones and The Masters.
A world of unconditional love.
As our energies blend
there is an unsettling moment.
A moment of energies adjusting
into the union of balance and harmony
Our oneness pulsates
in the pure, white light,
creating peace, joy, love, and harmony.
That very special form
I see vibrates into reality.
As I gain clarity,
I see myself
as a spiritual warrior
in the pure ,white light
as a diamond essence
of my soul-energy.

HO

THE GLOW

What once was
My once joyful inner being
The passion of my soul has surfaced
like the radiance of the sun.
I am aglow
in the color of yellow
walking in the light
with each and every step
making me lighter and brighter.
My aura is sending vibrations of love and acceptance.
I feel joy and peace within.
Things are different now.
My heart chakra is opening up
feeling the pain, fears, and burdens of all
glowing with the understanding
that the strength on the outside may be tears and fears on the inside
My heart is filling with
Kindness and compassion,
Gentleness and forgiveness,
Peace and happiness,
Love and joy.
I feel the beginning of a new awakening.
Death and Rebirth
kindling fires within;
my heart is open.
My words are softer and kinder,
my intuition is energized and revealing truths.
my crown is aglow in a pure, white light
Great Spirit is calling and revealing my spirit within.
I feel the warmth and love of the pure, white light.
My body is tingling all over
filling up with peace, joy, and happiness.
Walking and talking in balance within and without
harmonized, restored, empowered, and free;
I feel the glow of my spiritual energy.

HO

KNOWN ENCOUNTERS

Sometimes life is full of surprises.
Surprises meant to be.
Encounters of joy thru acquaintances
that meet destinies calling.
Times of above are now times of below.
I call on the raven for the answers in The Void.
And the answers are given by the grounding spirit of the eagle.
Great Spirit, I thank you for your lessons and blessings.
Also for the people you bring into my life.
One never knows who our Shaman Sisters are.
But we know who we are, thru energy.
The energy of love, purity, peace, joy, and happiness,
The Godliness and Spirit of Soul,
are our connections to sisters now in the millennium and forever.
God, open our eyes.
Cleanse our hearts and souls.
for the awakening of the feminine side.

FRIENDSHIP

What is a friend?
A loving and supporting person,
they're there whenever you need them.
Mind, body, and soul
someone you can count on.
No matter what the reason.
No matter what the time.
Good times, bad times, and those times in between.
Through tears, depression, despair, and hopelessness
to peace, joy, laughter, love, freedom, balance and harmony.
Recognizing the moments of
self-awakening, self-discovery, self-transformation and self-empowerment
brought me feelings of respect and honor;
Praise given for jobs well done,
support and love given at all times
no matter what.
What are the qualities of a true friend?
They are:
      Loving, caring, and supportive;
      Calm, patient, and understanding;
      Gentle, kind, and compassionate;
      Non-judgmental, objective, and forgiving;
      Honest, respectful, and truthful.
A friend gives clarity to all issues in a positive manner,
always remaining truthful in a gentle way.
Understanding that soft words spoken
in a way
opens up the heart and soul
so the real matter is revealed.
Listening is a tool for communication,
Loving no matter what,
Letting you grow at your own pace with guidance and understanding,
Are all tools for a good friendship.
A friend;
      Loves you without being attached
      And accepts what is.
That's what a true friend is.

HO

Marva Samuels

Marva Samuels

SISTERHOOD

Sisterhood is the awakening of the feminine side.
Feelings of heavy burdens left dormant.
Here, in the environment of a safe place,
we've unlocked and shared our heavy hearts,
even without the complete unity of the clan.
We have met with success
because every step is a triumph.
Maidens lift and open your arms to Father Sky;
ask for Deliverance and Peace.
Take part in earth walks
to assist with the grounding Spirit of Mother Earth.
Feel your change of direction and creative spirit.
Open up your heart chakra;
feel the rhythm of your heartbeat
with the rhythm of Mother Earth.
Unity is balance.
Can't you feel it?
Maidens, The Wolf is Calling.

HO

Marva Samuels

RITES OF PASSAGE

Sometimes moving on brings on emotions.
Emotions of excitement, joy, and fear of changes;
stepping up to a higher level means
more responsibilities, time, discipline, focus, and self-actualization.
Time means patience, understanding, assertiveness, and stamina.
Extending of self to others,
to meet a goal that you have already accomplished.
It's time to pat you on the back for a job well done,
and accept the moose totem with lessons and blessings of Great Spirit.
Let your emotions flow.
Feel the excitement of your inner energy light up and glow.
Let your eyes dance and cry tears of joy.
It's been nine years of dedication.
Not only through you but also through others who have also carried the torch.
ow you have passed it on to others.
The millennium is here.
And now it is time.
to step into the glow of your Rites of Passage.

HO

FREEDOM

Freedom is peace at last.
It is soaring to great heights like the eagle.
flying up, above, and beyond the heavens
venturing through the darkness of hate,
sadness, burdens, challenges, blockages, and negativity.
Pain carries such a heavy toll that is difficult to let go.
Even today we need permission to let go.
It's okay. Let it go.
You are safe now. They can't hurt you. I'll comfort and protect you. These words are such a comfort and mean so much to me.
Deep within our heart and soul we cry for autonomy.
For the ability to stand firm and tall
to make choices on our own and be accountable.
Where is your authentic self?
Can you take me home?
Liberate me from the pain?
Let me see the fun in life again?
Remember how we used to swing so high
laughing and giggling with such ease
going higher and higher;
swinging to great heights
brought such freedom.
Freedom of letting go of the baggage
for a sense of lightness and pure delight.
Feel the ease of twirling in a circle
dancing in the moonlight
jumping up and down.
Find your rhythm.
Understand you have free will.
Listen and be still.
Let your heart and soul do the talking.
Hear your truth.
Honor your truth.
Be your truth.
Speak your truth.
Truth will set you free.
When you reach your home of divine peace, joy, and
happiness, surround yourself in a pure, white light.
Embrace yourself with love.
Give thanks to the Goddess.
Feel your freedom and welcome yourself home
by saying, at last,
I'm free to be me.

HO

Marva Samuels

IS IT REALLY ME?

Is it really me?
Authentic versus inauthentic,
Truth versus un-truth,
Joy versus sadness,
Vulnerability versus safety.
Where is my strength and power? How and when did I let go? Really,
tell me the truth.
Who am I?
You have always been yourself, lost for many years,
creating walls of blockages
walking in fear and deception
playing games with emotions
unhappy within and without, never satisfied.
Always complaining and spreading negative thoughts and energies,

Two years,

My spiritual journey has awakened and enlightened my heart and soul
for qualities I thought I was portraying, but now I can stand tall and firm.
Understanding my soul at birth is my soul now; it has never left me and it has never
changed. And to reach my inner being of light, meditation, silence, and stillness are needed.
Finally I understand,
taking someone's power also means giving away some of one's power.
Fear as a victim, also brings fear to the offender.
In that moment of realization I began to laugh and actually felt joy

Time wasted,

Living in fear and deception
All the time my strength and power
Living within my heart and soul
Waiting and waiting.
What time is it?
Time for your authentic self to shine within and without
Time to awaken the energies of my heart and soul.
Time to listen to the voices within.
Time to take a new breath of life.
No longer a victim
Vulnerable and open to receive
Death and Rebirths.
Who am I?

A new woman,

My warrior carrying the Light,
my maiden reflecting in the Moon,
blending in One, creating the brilliance and radiance of the Sun,
finally standing on my truth,
full of love, joy, kindness, compassion and forgiveness,
being my authentic self.

HO

I AM

Being is I Am.
What is *I AM*?
I AM is my authentic self.
It is the essence of my soul.
My being with God and the Goddess
and my being at birth.
No sins.
No blockages or challenges.
Love in its purest state.
Positive energy flowing everywhere
my mind, body, and soul
full of love and peace
joy radiantly beaming within and without.
Nothing really matters because everything is as is.
Surrender and acceptance is the key
to unlocking the door of freedom and empowerment.
Being is *I AM*.
What is *I AM*?
Love, love, love
shining like the purest diamond
feeling the stillness and joy within
bridging the gap between Mother Earth and Father Sky
connecting the soul to the Goddess Head.
Love in its deepest form.
The heartbeat pulsating to the beat of the drum.
My soul-energy activated
seeking the highest energy.
Or should I say,
energy in its purest form?
Creating a rainbow shining radiantly in shades of many colors
making the diamond beam the beauty of the soul,
filling my heart with love, joy, peace, happiness
making my heart shine with compassion, kindness, and forgiveness.
All my energy is flowing in balance and harmony
because I am one with The Goddess,
Being is I AM.

I AM WHOLE

I am woman for my loving, nurturing, and caring soul
and for my tender loving caresses
here in my heart and soul.
I feel the emotions bursting with joy.
My soul emerging from within to without
discovering my self-love
detaching and loving
acceptance of self and others as is.
Letting go of fixed ways and persistent complaints
unobtainable visions are now available.
The possibilities unlimited
Transformation and energy alive
Energy soaring,
Illumination and clarity in the forefront
Innocence and trust no longer an issue
Truth from within now truth from without
Wisdom creating the joy and peace I AM.
Great Spirit my guide and my salvation
All-knowing and understanding
Goddess above All
The Mother and Father of the Universe.
Here in my new found freedom
the Moon reflects in the mirror
her brilliance and radiance
expanding to wholeness
celebrating my many blessings
feeling my feminine energies.
I finally understand
I Am Whole.

HO

BACK TOGETHER

Alone and afraid
With many fears of the past
Never letting go
Holding on
Carrying the dull light of many wounds
Comfortable in the hell I'm in.
Anger and rage,
Sadness and depression,
Frustration and defeat,
Alone and afraid
The secret is silenced.
Never spoken
only felt with the tightness and twisting sensation of the solar plexus
Broken-hearted
Tired, so tired
Wanting to be free
Asking Great Spirit for freedom and enlightenment
Slowly seeing the light grow stronger
Blockages and challenges are overcome.
Negative thoughts now positive energy
The past now the present
Present now the present
Living now in the present, creating the future
Lost souls returning and reconnecting
Uniting as one
Feeling love and joy again
Breathing a new breath of life
Because now,
I'm back together.

HO

AGREEMENTS

What is an agreement?
Agreements harmonizes the soul,
verbal or written words that bond a contract
words made to accommodate one and/or others.
Hopefully words of self-healing,
transformation of self in the forefront;
change is real.
Remain true to your authentic self.
Focus on what needs to be healed.
Remain positive with high energy,
full of the pure, white light.
Let it fill your heart and soul
with the radiance, brilliance, and purity of the diamond.
Never changing
remaining the same during sunlight or moonlight
always with the eye on the prize,
agreements for self-improvement, self-healing, and self-transformation,
Seek the Goddess within. Go forward. Advance.
Accept what is.
Be flexible like the willow.
But remain true to yourself.
See the change in yourself.
Words have meaning.
Have integrity.
Be honest in a kind, gentle manner.
Never assume,
Always do your best.
Connect your mind, body, and soul to the God Head.
Seek that inner-self.
that is one with Great Spirit.
Agreements are made
to let the love and joy burst in song
creating balance and harmony
and growth along the journey
So
surrender, release, and move forward.
Don't forget to laugh along the way.

LETTING GO

Letting go, letting go, letting go
so hard to do.
The bond of mother and child
that relationship of nurturing, caring and loving emotions
years of guidance and protection
always supportive
advice to always do your best, no matter what.
Success comes not in the winning, but in how you won.
Lessons of respect, honor, and trust are taught
for the importance of understanding self and others.
Tolerance of the utmost;
not all people are alike,
but we must love and respect them no matter what.
Our journey must always be of positive energy.
Then, one day, things change.
Our children are maturing.
Moving forward along their path.
Independence.
Rocking the bond
Children making their own decisions,
taking responsibility, moving on.
Self-awakening and self-discovery in the forefront,
transformation taking place.
Letting go, letting go, letting go,
so hard for a Mother to do.
The flow, on occasion, feeling like forceful waves,
emotions high,
self-awakening for Mother,
Your child is moving forward.
It's time to let go.
Our children are their own pathfinders.
The journey has now begun for them.
So Mother,
Step back
so I can move forward.
and our love can continue to grow.
Letting go, letting go, letting go.

HO

OPEN TO RECEIVE

Being opened to receive
has placed me in a position
that makes me free.
No one to interfere
or try to take the place
of being my intermediary
between Great Spirit and me.
My spiritual journey
has opened me up
allowing me to be free
with the understanding
that my connection to Great Spirit is between Him and me.
This found freedom has made me thankful.
I give thanks and gratitude
because my prayers have been answered.
My visions are alive.
Full of energy,
bursting with color and symbols
giving meaning and understanding
Be Still.
Be Silent.
Listen to your inner voices
give you the message or messages you need to hear.
To flow in balance and harmony
along your journey,
open up to receive
and Great Spirit will fill you with the pure, white light,
heal and empower you
and set you free.

HO

BALANCE AND HARMONY

Let me flow in rhyme and rhythm.
Swinging up
then swinging down
balance is the middle ground.
Let me walk in balance and harmony.
In the distance I hear the sounds,
the sound of the beating drums;
immediately, my heart beats and flows to the rhythm of the drums.
This connection grounds me to Mother Earth.
Feeling her nurturing and loving caresses,
made me slow down and pace myself.
Be Still.
Be Silent.
Listen.
Hear the voices.
Here in this space I felt serenity.
A feeling of pure love and joy
as my body began to tingle and relax;
nothing really mattered.
Because everything is as is.
As my body filled completely with peace and joy,
I felt the Rhapsody of Love.
And my body flowed with the rhythm of Mother Earth.
Finally, walking in balance and harmony,
my being and aura radiated energy of unconditional love.
Positive energy
As I walked The Sacred Path of Beauty
in balance and harmony.

HO

Searching Soul For Truth and Light

A NEW BREATH OF LIFE

Years and years of passing judgments,
using old values to set standards.
Social and environmental norms
created my world.
A world of negative energy
with attitudes, fears, and lies;
judging people by the worth of Man,
an unworthy Man at that.
Thanks to Great Spirit I have shed my old ways.
Transformation,
with a new breath of life,
Death and Rebirth,
I feel my soul.
It's a loving, nurturing, and caring essence,
full of truth, honesty, and respect, wisdom, and gratitude.
My authentic self shines and glows a radiant, pure light
of purity and wisdom.
Energy vibrates,
connecting my soul to The Goddess Head,
filling me with unconditional love,
enlarging and pulsating my aura,
healing my heart and soul,
energizing my being with;
    Love and joy,
    Peace and happiness,
Creating my healing
and unity with Great Spirit.
Law is:
    UNIVERSAL LAW vs GOD'S LAW
Answers to come from above
trust and faith in Great Spirit
and all needs will be met.
My soul is fearless, powerful, and honest
with a gentle, kind, loving, compassionate, and forgiving heart
A new breath of life
with a soul that has been
Transformed, Restored, and Empowered.

HO

THE DOVE

The dove
Life spirit
Symbol of love, peace, and purity
Feminine energy
Representing growth and maturity
A gift of the soul
A light of the Spirit
Sacred Mother Goddess
The dove teaches lessons of love.
    Love Is To Be Happy With One.
    Love connected my totems with the
Strength, power, and leadership of the lion,
Grace, innocence, and beauty of the swan,
Accomplishments, self-esteem, and wisdom of the moose,
Record keeping, wisdom, and music of the whale,
Magic, creation, and ceremony of the raven,
Freedom, illumination, and healing of the eagle,
Stamina, strength, and pacing of the elk,
Dream weaving, protection, and creativity of the spider.
And the Sacred Law, truth, renewal, and transformation of the crow
    My guardianship
To the loving soul I AM.
Within and without
sharing, caring, and loving with all.
Always,
my soul, life spirit
Emerging with the love of the dove
Safe journey.

HO

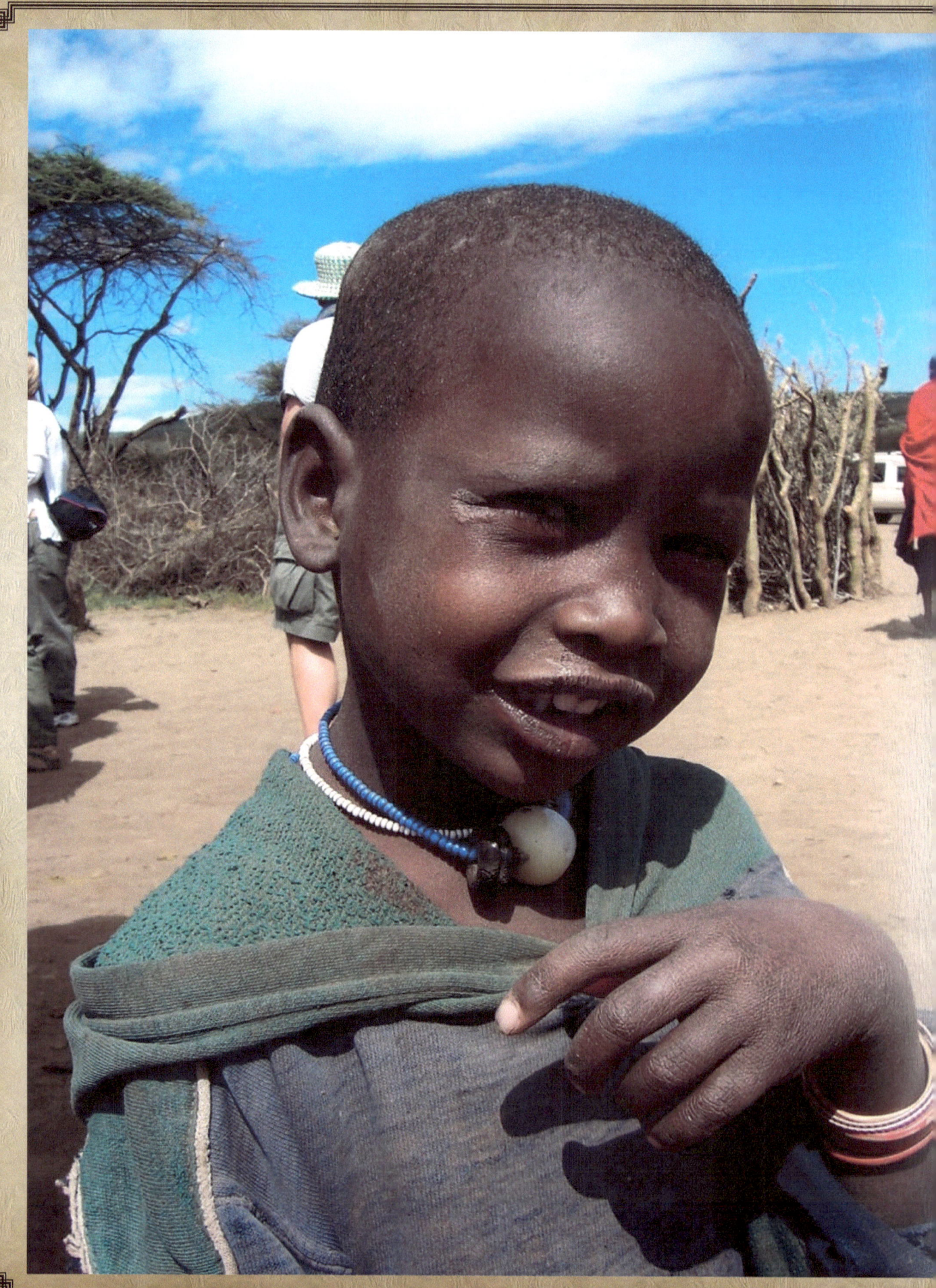

WHEN I WAS A CHILDS

When I was a child
I screamed, yelled, and hollered
When I was a child
I begged to be seen and heard
When I was a child
Attention I sought
When I was a child
There were lesson to learn
When I was a child
I cried to be understood.
But now
I'm grown.
Lessons in hand
Blessings and abundance from above
The Creator above all,
the inner flames aglow.
I glowed in radiance
Self-empowered.
Transformed.
Lessons in hand
I watch and listen
for all I can.

HO

Marva Samuels

AFRICA

Africa! Africa! Africa! My homeland once unknown and forgotten,
now, alive and vibrant.
A land of beauty, beautiful people and beautiful land
A place of peace and serenity
A spirit of peace and joy
A homecoming with a loving *Welcome Home*.
Brotherhood and Sisterhood, coming together as one Family, Tradition,
Friendship, Values, and Principles,
are strongly felt with the life energies of love, peace, joy, and
happiness. This African and kindred spirit:

> Love and Happiness
> Peace and Joy
> Balance and Harmony

Brought together tears of awakening and discovery with a profound healing.
My heart chakra wide opened, ready to receive, vulnerable to all there is,
happy to be home, feeling the grounding spirit of Mother Earth.
I walked feeling the loving spirit of Father Sky,
I prayed, as I meditated in silence.
I prayed;
For my connection to Great Spirit, my ancestors, my homeland and my
people. I reflected back on;

> African culture
> Slavery Bondage
> Emancipation
> The Struggle
> Higher Education
> Work-force
> Charity

I cried for the haves and the have nots.
For the Creator's Greatest love

> Love of God
> Love of self
> Love country

Africa
> My home
> My love
> My spirit

Africa!

Africa!

Africa!

HO

SISTERS OF THE DANCE

Sisters Of The Dance:
A time of loving, caring, and sharing together
A time of enrolling in the possibility of vulnerability
A time to open up and receive lessons and blessings.
Safe and comfortable in Sacred Circle,
A time to release our fears and inauthentic self
crying while releasing our burdens and challenges
knowing and understanding it is all right to be our authentic self
letting our emotions flow without interruption
feeling a sudden freedom of being alive
with a new breath of life,
so happy
full of peace and joy
in this environment of unconditional love
Great Spirit is glowing.
With our prayers
prayers of unity and equality, truth and honesty, trust and innocence, and clarity and understanding
for the highest good of mankind,
To end suffering of women and children
To end the misuse of Mother Earth
To end the dysfunctional family
To end the wars in the world
Sisters Of The Dance:
A time of uniting our feminine energies with Mother Moon
A time of love, peace, joy and happiness
living in balance and harmony
as we flow and glow together
in the Unity of Sisterhood.

HO

Searching Soul For Truth and Light

JOY AND RADIANCE

Joy is such a pleasure
I feel in my heart.
That special way,
the special way that makes me feel aglow.
My spirit fills with such delight
energizing and tingling all over my body,
making me relax in a state of peace and joy;
Nothing can be more fulfilling
than the complete sense of radiance.
The rays of the sunshine are glowing with brilliance
making me happy for each and every breath.
Thankful Great Spirit
has given me time to enjoy the beauty of self and universe
Seeing the energy change within means
Seeing the energy change without.
Sharing and caring with others
My newfound delight
begins a deeper understanding
of the environment, the community, and the universe.
Joy manifests the beauty of one's spirit
helping one connect to the Oneness and Godliness of Self
This powerful energy
creates love and beauty of all things.
Great Spirit,
let me rejoice in the glow of joy.
Such a feeling of pure delight
dancing, singing, smiling, and laughing
makes my spirit glow
in the warmth of
Joy and Radiance.

HO

TOLERANCE

Who are you?
Who am I?
We are human beings,
tolerant of each other,
no matter what color, race, religion, or creed
We are:
Non-judgmental
Non-assuming
Our words are our truth
so let our hearts and souls shine!
Striving for our higher selves
lets our authentic energy flow
Truth, honesty, and integrity
Flowing softly and gently
We are:
Full of love, compassion, forgiveness, and kindness
Expressing our love, joy, peace, and happiness together
Tolerance,
Divine Guidance,
Helping with our Spiritual Healing
fills us with a golden light-energy
Connecting us with Great Spirit
fills our hearts and souls with One Love.
Now, you love me
And I love you
Because,
We are:
Tolerant of each other

HO

WE ARE ONE

Feel me, Feel me
Go ahead
Touch me, Touch me
No need to hesitate.
Pinch me
Ooh that hurts
Let me pinch you.
Funny hey?
I feel what you feel
so we are all the same.
We are humans together
commonalities with all six senses
We see, feel, hear, smell, speak and perceive as humans, on all, one or more planes.
What do you mean?
A solid foundation consists of;
physical, mental, emotional, and spiritual planes
our differences are the environment, social, and economical status,
religion, race, culture, and language that creates who we are.
Meaning we live in a world of many different perceptions
some for the good of all mankind some for the good of none
The range is vast.
But our common bond remains our six senses
We can change.
The struggle might be hard
Truth is the answer.
So have faith and believe in Great Spirit.
Surrender all, not only for yourself but for the good of all mankind.
Pray for the Universe,
seek your higher self in the pure, white light
reclaim your strength and power
and follow your guided path.
Go amongst your brothers and sisters
Yes; my people, your people, all people because we are all related.
Walk and speak your truth,
Teach as The Divine has spoken, so we can come together in love, peace, joy and happiness
Walk in balance and harmony and be free and whole again,
living under one roof in the House of Great Spirit
In this Universe, so that the Rainbow Tribe Vision is a reality,
We strive to be whole and empowered again
so go forth wise Woman;
there is much to be done.

                          HO

PEACE AT LAST

Here in the land of plenty
beauty is portrayed through money, power, and ego.
The greater the estate and greater your worldly possessions
the richer you feel.
But unfortunately,
financial riches do not bring the peace and happiness one needs.
Fear of not having, not doing, and not performing
brings on negativity, with many burdens to lift;
with these burdens freedom never exists.
Depression and unhappiness are felt at home
while the mask of many faces is shown to the world.
So now, in the millennium,
I surrender myself to Great Spirit.
I cleanse my body, soul, and mind
by reaching back into past lives and dissolving burdens,
and lifting my spirit to a lighter and brighter me.
I cleanse my body with herbs to remove parasites and toxins,
to assist Great Spirit in my purification of mind, body, heart, and soul
I go within to reach the Oneness and Godliness of Self
To balance my male and female side and bond in marriage
for unity of love, peace, joy, and happiness
In this time of,
The Fifth World of Peace and Enlightenment
The vision of The Rainbow Tribe and Wise Women will be a reality,
and the howls of the wolf will be loud and plenty
because women will howl and sing
the teachings of the wolf
and bring to the people of the world
the Peace of the Universe
with The Blessings of Great Spirit.

HO

THE KEY OF LIFE

Where is the key? Who has the key?
Does anyone know where the keys are?
My inner-being is crying to get out.
Why am I so misunderstood?
Nobody listens, Nobody cares,
Who has the time? Who has the time!!!
In this stressful world
An accumulation of rules, regulations, and
laws Creates fear, challenges, and
uncertainties Yet they say my world is safe.
Great Spirit,
give me guidance and understanding.
My child the key is:

       Truth and Honesty
       Respect and Gratitude

Shed your outer shell layer by layer.
Release your burdens.
Center and ground yourself.
Connect with Great Spirit.
Let your inner being shine and glow radiantly.
Pray, and your needs will be met.
Meditate for clarity and understanding. Share
for guidance and humanity.
Play for peace of mind and joy.
Where is the key? Who has the key?
Child, you have the key
Unlock the door.
Release your burdens to Great Spirit.
Open up to receive.
Let your blessings and abundance flow. Seek,
And your needs will be met
With love, guidance, and understanding.
Forgiveness and compassion,
Gives,
Joy, peace, happiness, and laughter
So child, find the key,
Unlock the door
Open up to receive,
So you can
Glow and flow radiantly.

HO

IN GOD WE TRUST

As in the Christian religion one needs only
the faith of a mustard seed to have prayers
answered by God.
In the New Age spirituality one needs only
the flicker of the flame within
to awaken the spiritual growth
of the Oneness and Godliness of Self.
Open up your heart and feel the light
feel the glow of love, peace, joy, and happiness
as it caresses your body,
this feeling within also can be the feeling without.
Knowing with God your journey is unlimited,
limitations now are in the past.
Touching your heart and soul
God gives spiritual awakening, stability of relationships, love of all people,
and riches in abundance of all things.
God meets all needs.
For those who seek The Oneness and the Godliness of Self.
Seek your higher self
by having faith and trust in God.
and all your prayers will be answered.

HO

Vocabulary Words

1- Great Spirit -The Creator or the source
2- Great Mystery – Original source
3- Void – Mystery, darkness
4- Lamb of God – Jesus Christ
5- Father Sky – sky and all things within
6- Mother Earth – essence of feminine energy, birth of creation, earth energy
7- Drum- internal timing, rhythm
8- Rainbow Tribe – all nations
9- Oneness and Godliness of Self – connect to soul
10- Spiritual - connection to God, for some connection to soul
11- Four Directions – harmony and balance, lessons
    A – West – Meditation, beginning
    B – East – Clarity, Light
    C – South – Growth, spontaneity, innocence
    D – North – Renewal, revitalizer, wisdom
12 – Sacred Path – Spiritual journey, respective path
13 – I AM – One's soul
14 – Whirling Rainbow – Unity, wholeness, peace
15 – Kundalini – electrical current that runs up spine, extremities
16 – Charkas – energy or forces of swirls
17 – Grandmothers- Women medicine born from the families who refused to live on the reservation after the Trail of Tears. They settled in Mexico.
18 – Elder – First nation
19 – Clan Mother – Spirit Teachers
20 – Eternal flame – light within
21 – Masters – guides of a higher spiritual power
22 – Sky Nation – birds
23 – Creature being – animals
24 – Standing People – trees
24 – Totems – animal spirits
25 - Medicine Man – Healer of the village or tribe
26 - Long Dance – sisters of the tribe dance and drum from dusk to dawn, praying for needs of the tribe and world
27 - Kiva – going deep within the earth surrounded by rock formation – place of inner reflection
28 - Evolution Day – Birth Day
29 – Shamanism – Healer that goes into altered state of mind to heal
30 – Medicine Wheel – circle lessons to complete Native American road or way
31 – Death Arrow – ridding oneself of old habits and old way

Cont'd

32 – Act of power – become empowered
33 – Soul Retrieval – Reclaiming of power, return to wholeness
34 – Fifth World of Peace- A Navajo Legend where the people are of earth which some call Many Colored Earth
35 – Lion – strength, power, leadership
36 – Swan – grace, innocence
37 – Moose – accomplishments, self-esteem, wisdom
38 – Whale – record keeper, music
39 – Raven – magic, creation, ceremony
40 – Eagle – freedom, illumination, healing
41 – Elk – stamina, strength, pacing
42 – Spider – dream weaving, protection, creativity, weave the web
43 – Pelican – renewed buoyance, unselfish
44 – Parrot – sunshine, color of healing
45 – Coyote – jokester, hidden wisdom
46 – Bear – awakening power of unconsciousness
47 – Black Panther – reclaiming one's true power, ferocity
48 – Wolf – guardianship, loyal to pack, great sense of family
49 – Crow – secret magic, creation of dark black given birth to new day
50 – Hummingbird – joy
51 – Duck – emotional comfort and support
52 - Dolphin – common communicator of sound and rhythm
53 – Black – mystery, protection, power, deep meditation
54 – White – purity, cleansing, truth
55 – Gold – truth, power, good healing, service to others
56 – Silver – active, energizer
57 – Red – passion, energy, strength
58 – Orange – relationship to external world, needs and satisfaction of the physical body
59 – Yellow – sunshine, creativity, happiness
60 – Green- money, luck, fertility, healing, nature, self-love
61 – Blue - spirituality, intuition, calming
62 – Indigo – psychic ability, healing, relaxation, spiritual truth
63- Purple – power both earthly and spiritual, royalty
64 – Pink - unconditional love, friendship
65 – Brown – color of earth, material success, concentration, study, common sense
66 – Gray – sorrow
67 – Turquoise – protection strength, communication

Marva Samuels

Within the covers of this book is my spiritual journey of self-discovery, self-awakening, self-transformation, and self-actualization. Along the journey I have captured emotions that touched my heart and soul.

Together with my photos, I expressed my deepest thoughts of my feelings within. Every poem was guided by a word, a phrase, and or a sentenced from God. His presence was made known by whispering words that awakened my spirit and encouraged me to write a given theme. God's whispers did not stop; until I began to create words into a poem. Each theme has a spiritual healing or thought that runs deep within my heart and soul. It is these healings and thoughts that hopefully will touch your heart and soul, and give you the truth you seek.

Within the light of God, renders the truth of life. Seek your truth and light within by searching your soul. God is waiting at anytime to guide you, and give you love and understanding of yourself, to make you whole.

Now is the moment to shed your negative energy and move forward to positive experiences. Be motivated to seek your power and effective with experiences to obtain your lessons, blessing, and abundance.

Accept all that comes your way in a positive manner since there are no limits. All things are possible. I hope this book gives you motivation to move forward.

Remember, now is the moment of your power, power comes from within, love is to be happy within, and effectiveness is the measurement of truth. Safe journey.

Biography

My name is Marva Samuels and I am an author and a poet. I was born and raised in Montreal, Quebec, Canada. Presently, I live in Sacramento, California with my son, daughter-in-law and 3 grandchildren.

I started writing in 1976 and stopped in 1977 due to young adult-hood stress. As time progressed, things changed. So while studying Native American Spirituality, The Wolf Clan in 1998, I started writing again. Now, instead of hard, negative prose I wrote soft positive prose with the subject matter remaining the same; awaking, discovery, transformation, and actualization. I have included two of my poems from 1976: *Egotism* and *Soul Within*. Plus two poems my son created: *Goodbye* and *From A Boy, To A Man*.

I enjoy music; contemporary and smooth jazz, R&B, blues, soft hip-hop revealing social and political injustices, symphony and opera.

For more information contact author at email, *marvasamuels1@att.net*.

www.ingramcontent.com/pod-product-compliance
Lightning Source LLC
Chambersburg PA
CBHW041510220426
43661CB00047B/1522